GIRL TALK, GOD TALK

GIRL TALK, GOD TALK

Why Faith Matters to Teenage Girls—and Their Parents

Joyce Ann Mercer

JOSSEY-BASS
A Wiley Imprint
www.josseybass.com

Published by Jossey-Bass
A Wiley Imprint
989 Market Street, San Francisco, CA 94103-1741—www.josseybass.com

Jossey-Bass books and products are available through most bookstores. To contact Jossey-Bass directly call our Customer Care Department within the U.S. at 800-956-7739, outside the U.S. at 317-572-3986, or fax 317-572-4002.

Scripture quotations are from Revised Standard Version of the Bible, copyright 1952 [2nd edition, 1971] by the Division of Christian Education of the National Council of the Churches of Christ in the United States of America. Used by permission. All rights reserved.

Jossey-Bass also publishes its books in a variety of electronic formats. Some content that appears in print may not be available in electronic books.

Library of Congress Cataloging-in-Publication Data

Mercer, Joyce.
    Girl talk, God talk : why faith matters to teenage girls-and their parents /
Joyce Ann Mercer. —1st ed.
        p.   cm.
    Includes bibliographical references and index.
    ISBN-13: 978-0-7879-7594-4 (cloth)
        1. Teenage girls—Religious life.   2. Teenage girls—Conduct of life.   I. Title.
    BV4551.3.M47   2008
    248.8'33—dc22
                                                            2007046926

Printed in the United States of America
FIRST EDITION
HB Printing   10 9 8 7 6 5 4 3 2 1

CONTENTS

For Sarah Elizabeth
Spirited Girl, Gift of God
and always,
my Sarah-Bear

ACKNOWLEDGMENTS

GRATITUDE IS THE NATURAL CONSEQUENCE OF WRITING, at least for me, because writers depend on so many others and need so much assistance to perform their craft. I begin with gratitude to the young women of the Youth Theological Initiative (YTI). For more than a decade, they have offered me and other adults at YTI the gift of their voices and stories, allowing us to listen to them and giving us permission to use their interviews in research and writing as we work to know more about young people's religious lives. My gratitude, respect, and appreciation for their candor and thoughtfulness in these conversations is enormous. I have grown in my life and faith by walking alongside them through these interviews over the years.

Listening to the young women at YTI also renews my gratitude for adult women and men—especially Rose Scudder, Billy McLean, Ramona Clopton, and Diane Price—who listened to me with care when I was an adolescent girl, and who opened to me a living faith in which we could be part of God's transforming work of love and justice for all. Although I am not in frequent contact with any of them today, I remain grateful for their presence, their engaged modeling of faith, and their care during my adolescence that had and continues to have such an important impact on my religious life.

I am grateful to the directors, faculty, and research fellows of YTI, without whom this book would not have been possible, especially Don Richter, Faith Kirkham Hawkins, David White, James Fowler, and Dori Baker. Dori performed the unseen labor of reading most of these chapters in draft form. Her care for adolescent girls, along with her journalist's instinct to keep the sentences short and to the point, both found their way into these pages and made them better reading than would otherwise have been the case. Brad Wigger of Louisville Presbyterian Theological Seminary was instrumental in helping me to shift my frame of reference from that of a researcher working with interviews to a new role as the writer of this book.

I appreciate the students at Virginia Theological Seminary (VTS), who care about the religious lives of youth and have been conversation partners in classes, at lunch, and in chapel. Faculty colleagues at VTS graciously allowed me to vent my anxiety and stress over this project, which I brought with me when I moved here a year ago. They have also taken pleasure in the joys I have found in this work, and they have celebrated it with me in small ways. I especially thank those in the department of practical theology, who value the kind of writing to which this book aspires— writing for people who may or may not spend most of their time inside a seminary, but for whom the thoughtful practice of faith in everyday life matters greatly. Thanks to Barney Hawkins, Roger Ferlo, Jacques Hadler, Amy Dyer, George Kroupa, and Tim Sedgwick. And I have continuing gratitude for work and friendship with my former chaplain colleague David Berg, whose insights and whose knowledge of youth continue to inform my perspectives. Feminist friends and colleagues—especially Boyung Lee, Liz Heller, and Evelyn Parker—encouraged me to keep believing, across many interruptions and derailments of this project, that a book on the spiritual lives of adolescent girls was worth writing. Members of the Irish Breakfast Band, in Alexandria, Virginia, offer me breaks from all things academic and help recharge my energies through music in addition to their being all-around fun and interesting people. Thanks for waiting for me to find the music.

Writers need those others in their lives who are willing to humor them in moments of despair and put up with them through long periods of preoccupied absence from the rest of life. I am graced with many such people, but certainly first among them are members of my immediate family, including Sandy, our faithful old German shepherd, who warms my feet and my heart while I type late into the night. My marriage partner, Larry Golemon, lovingly brings me coffee every morning, whether or not he feels like doing so. He has kept our family afloat with meals, homework help, and endless carpooling during times when I was living holed up in my proverbial lonely writer's den. Some of those times have been especially long and difficult for him, and so I am grateful for care shown through the painstaking perseverance of getting through yet another day when I have not been particularly available to him or my family. My sons, Andrew and Micah, have cheered me on faithfully throughout—"Mama, what chapter are you writing now?"—and brought "boy energy" into my days at times when all this focus on girls threatened to become stupefying. My daughter, Sarah, in addition to the everyday encouragement I get just from waking up in the same house with someone so attentive to life, provides me with a personal stake in this book's subject matter as we move together into her adolescence. This book is dedicated to Sarah, with love beyond measure.

JOYCE ANN MERCER
Alexandria, Virginia
January 2008, Epiphany

PREFACE

POPULAR WISDOM HOLDS that authors inevitably write their own lives—that is, people who write books choose their subject matter from the things that matter or shape their lives rather than from some detached, objective interest in a topic. I cannot argue with that! I have spent most of my adult life working with adolescent girls in religious, clinical, or educational settings. Something about these girls inspires continual curiosity and interest in me about their ways of making sense of the world and their ways of dealing with the complexities of their lives today. Apart from my present-day interest in and connections with girls, however, the real genesis of this book is undoubtedly my own experiences of adolescence, a time of intense spiritual awareness and religious interest, of hopeful ideals passionately held, of important relationships, and of significant pain, struggle, and sometimes also deep joy in life.

Sorting Out How to Be Faithful

I recall my teen years as a time of impassioned religious curiosity. I felt a longing to make sense of the "big questions." What is the meaning of life? Does my life have a purpose, and if it does, what might that be? If God is good, why are so many people in pain and suffering? Does God care about my pain and suffering (and can God do anything about it)? Are the many religions of the world simply different expressions of the same cosmic reality, or is it more complex that that—and how can I best understand this multiplicity in relation to my Christian faith? What visions of goodness, wholeness, life, and relationships are most "real"? What values will most sensibly order my life—or, given what I think I believe, how should I try to live, both in immediate, everyday relationships and situations and in relation to the rest of the world, its people, and their needs?

These kinds of questions formed the landscape of my religious inquiry as a teenager trying to make sense of the larger world in which I lived and to craft a way of life that had meaning in such a world. And yet I often felt that most of the people around me were operating under a "don't ask, don't tell" policy when it came to the faith that I experienced as so central to my everyday life. Many adults seemed afraid to broach the subject of religion with me or other young people I knew. Were they afraid of saying the wrong thing? Were they trying to avoid having their comfortable or long-held religious perspectives unsettled, or even critiqued, by a questioning teenager? Whatever the cause of their silence, I recall very few adults in my life with whom I could express, discuss, and explore religious meanings.

And, unfortunately, this silence was not necessarily broken in my peer group of other teens. It was clear to me that my friends and acquaintances spent a great deal of time thinking about religious ideas, and many even engaged in faith practices as they participated in the activities of their churches or parachurch youth ministries (for example, nondenominational Christian organizations, such as Young Life, that are religious but not affiliated with any particular church). But talking about religious beliefs or spiritual practices, or acting too interested in church and youth-group activities, brought swift sanction in the form of negative labeling: the teenager stuck with a label like "Bible thumper" or "religious nerd" was on the fast track to social exclusion. In the culture of my adolescent years, it was good to be known as someone who went to a church. It was *not* good to be known as someone who really liked church or was interested in theological matters.

Sorting Out How to Be Female

I also recall my teen years as a time of considerable difficulty. Family relationships took on a new level of intensity, often of conflict. Some of my personal struggles mirrored the unsettled social context in which I lived. My adolescence extended from the late 1960s into the 1970s, and I lived near Richmond, Virginia, on the edge of the southern Bible Belt. These were the years of the end of the Vietnam War. They were also years of significant social shifts spurred by various movements for justice, such as the civil rights movement and the women's movement. An assortment of often contradictory images of women was coming my way, and it was especially hard for me to make sense of them.

Sometimes these images of women came in the form of song lyrics. One popular female vocalist crooned dreamy rock lyrics about being a "natural woman." At the same time, popular tunes by one male vocal group painted pictures of blissful domestic settings to which hard-working men came home to find their carefree female partners waiting for their return. On some level, my mind and body resonated with these songs; the music and words stirred sensual and passionate desires for connection and romantic relationships befitting the cultural images of womanhood into which my southern childhood had socialized me.

At the same time, though, amidst the plethora of changes taking place in women's roles and opportunities, I wondered what a "natural woman" really was, and how all this blissful domesticity on the radio would fit with my developing desire to make a difference in the world, a desire that, for me, had implicitly religious overtones, given my faith heritage in the Reformed tradition of Christianity. (This theological tradition stresses the idea that God calls all persons to give themselves to others in lives of service that work toward God's reign of love and justice for all.) There on the edge of the Bible Belt, I found myself surrounded by religious as well as cultural images of "authentic womanhood" that seemed rather limited in the "making a difference in the world" department.

It was all so confusing. After all, there were other images of women in currency at that time, and they contrasted with the romances of song lyrics. These images, carried over the airwaves on nightly newscasts, or making their appearance at dinner-table debates, showed women expanding the acceptable definitions of "female." Young women athletes were benefiting from the new Title IX legislation mandating girls' equal access to athletic programs in schools. Women were entering occupations that had been off limits to them. Women in faith communities were taking on public leadership roles as ordained ministers. Sorting out how to be female in such a time was exhilarating. It was also very hard work.

Being Faithful and Female

Of course, the years of my adolescence comprised a very different era from the present one. Sorting out what it meant to be female and Christian in that time and context was a task complicated by the seismic shifts in gender roles, and by the changing role of religion and religious organizations in society. But after years of talking and working with today's adolescent girls from all around the United States, I am convinced that if some issues and options are different now, the process of negotiating gender and religious meanings remains every bit as complex for them as it was for me.

Issues of gender and religion are not automatically or self-evidently intertwined. But as a teen trying to figure out how my faith was asking me to live, and with developmental processes all the while pushing matters of sexuality, gender role, and gender identity to the foreground, I found that gender issues were virtually guaranteed to have a religious dimension, too.

The same is true for young women today who identify with a faith group, especially girls from more conservative denominations.

A Story from My Past

As an adolescent, I was actively exploring connections between religious belief and personal and communal action, and my exploration included beliefs and actions informing the roles of women and men in society. My quest sometimes drew me into troubled waters.

Our local newspaper in Richmond sponsored what it called its Youth Advisory Board, and I was a member. We were a group of teens who gathered from time to time to hold a conversation about current events, and then the paper would print the transcript of our discussion as part of a feature on youth. One of these discussions was about sex roles and relationships between girls and boys. When the discussion turned to the different ethical standards for the sexual behavior of girls and boys, I made a bid for gender equality, suggesting a change in what was then the common expectation that the boy would foot the expenses on a date. If the girl paid her own way, I reasoned, that would remove the implicit but common expectation that she owed her date something in exchange, in the form of whatever sexual currency she possessed. Then she and her date would both be freed from unspoken power arrangements and obligations and could simply be present with each other on the same terms. That seemed to me like a more just and more ethical way to go on a date. I did not express this idea in explicitly religious terms, but it had certainly taken shape in conjunction with my emerging faith perspectives on human dignity, just relationships, and the connections between personal behavior and the social structures shaping human relationships.

When the story appeared in the paper, with my little three-line comment, a few people offered support and affirmation for my egalitarian perspective. But I also experienced a lot of name calling and taunting in the halls at school that week. "Look out, here comes the women's libber!" "Girls who can't get a date have to pay for a guy to take them out." Classmates passed notes to me asking why I didn't like being a girl, or why I wanted to mess things up for girls who liked having boys take care of them and pay their way. What astonished me most was the religious overtone of many of these critical taunts. It was suggested, for example, that if girls started paying their own way, they would grow up to be women who wanted to be the breadwinners in their households, and everyone knew that was against the teachings of the Bible. I even received two letters in the mail from adults who were troubled by what they saw as my suggestion that the God-given arrangement between men and women was problematic. Clearly, what I had seen as a perspective grounded in faith appeared to some as the antithesis of faithfulness.

Meanwhile, my mother, with whom I had a fairly intense and often conflicted relationship in those years, simply said, "Your idea sounds like a pretty good one to me. Besides, at least you were trying to figure out some different ways of doing things. Most of those other kids in the article just made it sound like everything is fine the way it is! It's not like God worked it all out ahead of time." And my pastor, shaking my hand as I left the Sunday service that week, quietly said, "I saw your comments in the paper. Good for you! I bet some people are giving you trouble about that one. It'll push some buttons. But you just keep on pushing—God might have a new thing coming for women and men in this world."

It is significant that my mother and my pastor were among those who stood with me, and they both expressed their support in a way that recognized the faith issues that were involved for me. Neither of them would have qualified for even auxiliary membership in the radical fringe of Richmond, Virginia, in the 1970s; both were fairly conventional in their relationships and viewpoints. But what they did involved something slightly different from simply offering agreement with my perspective on who should pay for a date, and why. (In fact, I am not even sure that either of them wholeheartedly agreed with me.) My mother and my pastor both affirmed my *quest* as well as the connections I was making between something as mundane as who paid for a date (including the power relations expressed in that arrangement) and the ways in which religion was used to structure gender relations at that time and in that place. Both of them, without much ado, honored my effort to make sense of being both a Christian and a teenage girl—to hold being faithful with being female.

Back to the Present

I offered this story from my past as a way of locating my personal stake in the connections among being an adolescent, being religious, and being female. Today, as an adult, I care, just as my mother and my pastor showed they did, about helping adolescent girls sort out the religious meanings that fund their lives, decisions, and vocations. And, given the continuing influence of gender-based societal norms, I am convinced that these issues often take shape differently for girls than they do for boys. Experiences such as the one I've just recounted helped to shape my lifelong interest in exploring and understanding how religion and gender find expression in adolescence, and my interest in thinking about the importance of adults who support or fail to support girls in quests involving both gender and religion, particularly the involvement of parents in the religious lives of girls. One outcome of these lifelong interests is that today in my work as a scholar and researcher of religious practices, adolescent girls are not simply interesting subjects of my research; instead, they hold a prominent place among the groups of people to whom I feel a special commitment of responsibility, support, and advocacy. As a result, I have spent much of my professional life working with adolescents—especially girls—and their families, in various efforts to contribute to their well-being and foster their thriving.

These days, as a member of the practical theology faculty at a Christian theological seminary, I teach seminary students about youth ministry and I conduct research on youth and ministries with youth. I am also a mother living with the imminent prospect (accompanied by no little trepidation) of parenting my own children through adolescence. I relate to teenagers as my neighbors, as my fellow and sister church members, and as members of the confirmation classes I teach from time to time. Earlier in my life, I was a clinical social worker in an adolescent medical clinic that served a diverse group of urban teens. I have been a pastor of a large midwestern congregation that included many teenagers. And for a number of years I served as chaplain in a chemical dependency treatment program for adolescents, helping young people address the spiritual and religious aspects of their recoveries from addiction, abuse, and grief. Throughout all these different kinds and contexts of my involvement with young people, I have marveled at the passion they bring to their desire to shape a worldview and a way of life that will make sense in relation to their encounters with God, with other people, with a complex world in pain, and with their own emerging sense of identity.

I said earlier that few adults in my adolescence were willing and able to talk with me about matters of faith. But there were some, and they were immensely important to my ability to navigate the rough waters and negotiate the tough topics of the teen years. This book is my effort to surface some of the concerns of girls who stand at the intersection of religion, gender, and family relationships, and to do so in a way that adults can hear and respond to, and that can ultimately support the spiritual lives of adolescent girls.

INTRODUCTION

KIT, A TALL GIRL with a quick sense of humor and a ready smile, talked to me for almost an hour about family relationships, passionately recalling her struggles growing up in a household where her parents' relationship was marked by conflict that sometimes escalated into violence between her parents. She spoke of her frustration with her parents' constant moves in search of "that place where we would magically turn into one big happy family." She cried when she described how alone she had felt the day she came home from school to find that her father had moved out without even saying goodbye. And she also spoke of caring relationships with teachers, of a best friend with whom she could share anything, and of her love and respect for her mother, "who got us through all that." She offered examples of music that helped her to express her innermost feelings and hopes, described the feeling of freedom and transcendence she got when snowboarding with her boyfriend, and, with anxiety edging her voice, worried out loud about how she would be able to finance a college education.

At the end of an hour of emotional interviewing, she and I decided to take a short break before continuing. I turned the tape recorder off, saying to her as we left the interview room together in search of a soda machine, "When we come back, let's turn to talk about your understanding of God and what your faith is all about these days." Without even the slightest pause, Kit retorted, "God and faith? That's what I *have been* talking about for the past hour!"

The Religious Lives of Girls

This book is about adolescent girls and how they think about, experience, and express spiritual and religious meanings in their lives. It is also a book about the connections between family relationships and the religious lives of girls. In particular, it is about the relationships that adolescent girls have with their mothers and fathers, their stepmothers and stepfathers, their "other mothers,"[1] and various other "parenting adults" whose practices of parental care can support girls' lives of faith.

In the complex and intense life of an adolescent girl, religion and faith often function as the glue that holds things together for her as she moves from the self she was in childhood to the person she is in the present and on to the self of an adulthood that waits just around the corner. And, like glue, which works invisibly, unseen except as it does its job of holding something intact, religion is for many girls an essential but largely unseen aspect of their ability to navigate between their selves and their worlds. At the same time, though, because faith is both a set of ideas and a set of practices forming a way of life, adults who want to know, understand, and support adolescent girls cannot ignore girls' religious lives.

Kit's story comes from one of many interviews I conducted with girls participating in the Youth Theological Initiative (YTI), a monthlong residential summer academy for rising high school juniors that was begun in the 1990s.[2] Fifty of these interviews form the basis of this book. Kit's remarks serve as a reminder that "girl talk" on faith may take place in relation to *any* aspect of life. It is not restricted to speech, ideas, or actions with explicitly religious content (for example, praying, church attendance, or reading the Bible), although it certainly may refer to those things.

Although she did not use much "God talk" in that first hour's conversation, I discovered later that Kit, at the age of seventeen, already had an extensive theological vocabulary. She had spent considerable time and energy reading and reflecting on the connections between hard times in her life and her beliefs about God, and she had long ago concluded that God was the force for good that made it possible for her and her siblings to survive the difficult years of which she spoke. Thus the idea that talking about having survived family struggles *already was* a way of talking about God that came easily to her.

Other girls find it more difficult to talk about faith, or to see their everyday experiences, problems, and questions in relation to religion, even though they readily identify themselves as having religious faith. They lack a vocabulary for naming the "big questions and worthy dreams"[3] that constitute religious imagination. They have grown up in a society where legal notions of the separation of church and state encourage them to view religion as a private matter, best not discussed in public for fear that it may be offensive or even illegal to do so. Unaccustomed to voicing religious perspectives, such girls are akin to those teens described as religiously inarticulate in Christian Smith and Melinda Lundquist Denton's empirical study on adolescent religiosity.[4] These girls claim that religion is important to them, and yet they are unable to identify in any detail what they believe or how religion matters in their lives.

Where's the Religion?

Contemporary psychologists and educators who study girls mirror this difficulty with talking about religion. My local bookstore provides a clear illustration of the erasure of religion and spirituality from most efforts to understand girls today. There, on an ever-expanding section of shelves, I can find numerous titles focused on adolescence, and even some that specifically concern girls. These books examine eating disorders, girls' self-esteem, and their relationships to their mothers. They address the buying power of "tween" and teen girls. They analyze the processes by which MTV and other elements of corporate America study trends in teens' music and apparel, only to package and sell these trends back to girls (and boys) in the form of something vaguely termed "youth culture." These books coach adults on how to save the lives and souls of adolescent girls who are at risk for what researchers call "de-selfing," or loss of the sense of identity and strong selfhood, upon entry into the teen years.

In the recent flurry of "girl literature" by psychologists and educators, there is virtually no evidence that religion is in any way significant for who girls are and how they live. For example, Daniel J. Kindlon, a psychologist best known for his work on adolescent boys (*Raising Cain*), says nothing in a new work—*Alpha Girls*, subtitled *Understanding the New American Girl and How She Is Changing the World*—about religion as a force in this amazing girl's life.[5]

A recent scholarly collection of research on adolescent girls, titled *Beyond Appearance: A New Look at Adolescent Girls,* contains chapters discussing the relational lives of girls, race and ethnicity, dating violence, health care, and sexuality. In more than four hundred pages of writing on girls, the only mentions of religion are brief and pejorative. The first comes in a reference to the "dominant White Christian culture" as promoting negative views of adult women that "make early adolescence difficult for many girls."[6] The second comes in a quick survey of evidence that religion supports some girls, evidence that is immediately discounted by the authors, who "question how adolescent girls are likely to become empowered by the very institutions that reinforce the more traditional roles of women in religious settings and in society."[7] On the one hand, such critiques are valuable in addressing the problematic aspects of religion in the lives of girls. It is true that religious institutions have played a role in social supports for women's subordination. That aspect shows up in some of the girls' interviews featured in this book, and it is addressed in this Introduction. On the other hand, though, the simplistic dismissing or complete ignoring of religiosity in the lives of girls seems to reflect an unfortunate ignorance of the many-faceted nature of religious beliefs and practices in the United States. Conservative talk-show Christianity, with its narrow and sexist understandings of women's roles in family and society, cannot be allowed to define religion for everyone. And yet researchers in psychology, such as the authors of the volume just mentioned, seem to accept this negative, narrow notion of Christianity. They appear oblivious to the reality that in the United States there are many Christian faith communities committed to the empowerment and thriving of girls and women.

Moreover, in their bias against religion, these researchers fail to recognize that for many young women religion operates as a simultaneously limiting or constricting force and also as a location of empowerment. Faith is not, as one young woman noted, "only one thing," either oppressive or liberatory. Faith communities, like other kinds of mediating social institutions in this country, may contribute to women's subordination on some levels while also, on other levels, being sites for emancipatory resistance. When researchers, fearful or unaware of the multiplicity of religion's presence in women's lives, neglect it in young women's experience, they ignore a vital but complex feature of these girls' lives. In the studies of girlhood by most educators and psychologists, the religious lives of girls are missing in action, even though many of these studies claim to offer newer, more complete understandings of the lives and selfhood of girls. Girls' religious lives are missing not because religion is unimportant to girls but because it is misunderstood by so many of those who study girls.

What these books do not seem to take account of is the significance of religious and spiritual experience in the lives of adolescent girls—the many ways spirituality and religion impact everything from self-esteem and body image to how girls deal with the pain in their lives and in the world. Furthermore, in most of the popular books on adolescence, the absence of explicit attention to matters of faith and religion suggests that parents, although they are or should be intensely concerned about virtually every other facet of their daughters' lives, find faith somehow off limits as a subject of parental interest, concern, or influence. Meanwhile, in congregations around the country, and in research among parents of teens, parents express the wish to understand and nurture the faith lives of their daughters, signaling the gaps between the experiences of girls (which include faith experiences), the desires of parents to support the faith development of their adolescent daughters, and existing studies about young women.

This book is my attempt to respond to those gaps. In describing some of the contours of the religious lives of adolescent girls and the diverse family relationships supporting them, I hope to contribute to a deeper understanding of the intersections among adolescence, faith, and being female. I hope to move toward a more complex view of adolescent girls, one that includes religious passions, convictions, actions, and meanings as central to the identities of these girls. It is also my hope that the connections I draw between girls, their religious lives, and their relationships with their parents will be helpful to parents who care about nurturing this key aspect of their daughters' personhood.

Everything Relates to Faith

What theologians, pastoral counselors, Christian educators, and sociologists of religion know from our studies of adolescents, and from the growing body of practical theological research with girls,[8] stands in stark contrast to this silence about religion in the social sciences. The girls with whom we work are constantly thinking, talking, and acting in relation to their religious understandings. For the girls in the YTI interview-study group, religious practices were not a neutral, insignificant aspect of their lives but were central to their self-understanding.

These girls made decisions about everything, from the clothing they purchased to their sexual activities, in relation to faith. Religion informed the ways they thought about and lived out their gender identities. It gave a sense of direction to their educational and career choices. Faith oriented them toward particular acts of service and drew them to join with others in support of such causes as animal rights, environmentalism, and children's access to health care. Their participation in faith communities often played a major role in supporting them through personal crises and difficulties. Their images of God and their religious understandings of how the universe works were in the process of being knit into overarching perspectives from which to live. Girls were engaged in a range of daily practices related to their religious perspectives. In short, religion was central to who they understood themselves to be—a vital feature of their everyday lives.

Could it be that this claim merely reflects the fact that when girls are in religious contexts (such as YTI, church camps, or church youth groups), they speak and act religiously? To be sure, such contexts do bring explicit religious language and practices to the fore. Girls who come to YTI are girls who, before they arrive, have already identified matters of faith and spirituality as significant in some way, so it is not unusual that we find religion to be significant in their lives. To put it differently, the group of girls who participated in these interviews was distinct from the general population of adolescent girls in one important way that bears noting: they were self-selected (girls apply to YTI) as being interested in faith talk and ready and able to engage in it. They did so at different levels of complexity and ability, and even with different degrees of comfort. In some cases, they engaged in faith talk while questioning the very basis of the beliefs they spoke about. But for each of these girls it can be said that religious stories, ideas, and practices constituted, in some sense, a worldview, a way of making sense of and understanding life. Their very identities were shaped by their sensitivity to and interest in spiritual matters, by their having a religious outlook on the world.

At the same time, however, it does not make sense to think that only those girls who show up at places like YTI or church youth groups have spiritually informed identities. We cannot generalize from the YTI interviews to comment on the religious lives of all girls, but it seems likely that at least some of the girls studied by psychologists and educators also have religious lives of significance. In adolescence, many girls work out their identities not in the absence of spirituality or religious faith but in integration with it. That is, spirituality and religion play a key role in who these girls are, and in who they see themselves becoming.

Despite the fact that their faith plays such a huge part in their lives, adolescent girls are not asked very often to talk about it. And when they do engage in such talk, their understanding of their own religious experiences may be discounted or not taken seriously. Consider these responses by two young women invited to talk about their faith perspectives:

> No one has ever asked me about this before. They want to know what kind of toothpaste I buy, or almost anything else, before they'll ask about my religion. Usually people just kind of assume that they already know what it means and how I live. They say, "Oh, she's a Baptist, she must read the Bible every day, not dance, and never kiss boys." But that's not what my religion means. If they asked me, I would tell them. It's a lot different than what they probably think.
>
> **—Althea**

> It might help if somebody would believe me for a change. . . . When I try to talk about my faith, I get these looks like "You can't be serious, that kind of thing doesn't really happen." Or they try to convince me that it means something else, that it's just psychological or something.
>
> **—Mary**

Such comments point to the difficulties a girl may face in speaking about her religious experiences and perspectives. She is asked about everything except her life of faith. Or, if her particular religious expressions do not fit the hearer's perspectives, she may find, as Mary did, that her experiences are discounted as unbelievable.

In fact, history even suggests that sometimes it may be dangerous for young women to disclose their religious perceptions, if we take as examples the persecution of young women in the Salem witch trials, or of martyred but later sainted young women like Joan of Arc, whose first religious visions came when she was twelve years old. Certainly, adolescent girls who talk about their religious experiences in the contemporary United States are less likely to experience physical persecution than these well-known historical figures. But Althea's and Mary's comments stand alongside many similar remarks by adolescent girls, all of them testifying to the fact that the faith lives of girls today continue to be trivialized or discounted, if they receive any attention at all.

In Their Own Words

How can we learn about the intimate religious lives of girls? Girls' experiences of relationship with God, their ways of living out their faith commitments, and the content of their most deeply held values and convictions hardly comprise the stuff of everyday social conversations in high school hallways. Similarly, for many girls, thoughts and feelings concerning relationships with parents may be reserved for late-night conversations in a sleepover with a best friend rather than shared with an adult seeking to learn about them. Admittedly, the topics that comprise this book's main focus are not easily accessible.

Given such difficulties in learning about girls, some people who study and write about adolescence prefer to learn about teens by using observation, by creating experimental situations to study behavior, or by analyzing media depictions of adolescents for themes and content deemed typical. But this book, in contrast to such approaches, is informed by the key conviction that one of the best ways to learn about the intricacies of girls' religious lives is to ask the girls themselves. I hold that in-depth, life-narrative interviews offer a valuable way of hearing and understanding the faith lives of girls, one that can't be ignored. In this book, therefore, the main source of information for exploring the intimate matters of spirituality, family relationships, and being female in these times is girl talk—the talk of girls themselves, as drawn from more than a decade of conversations and interviews with adolescent girls who shared their life stories and responded to invitations to talk about how they made meaning religiously.

"Meaning making" is a term I will use in this book to refer to the human process of making sense of reality. As human beings, we seek to know and understand our lives, our experiences, our world. People engage in meaning making when they reflect on life experiences or ideas and attempt to give meaning to or make sense of these things. The girls whose religious lives are the subject of this book agreed to tell their stories, responding to questions about being Christian, female, and adolescent in the United States in the years leading up to and inaugurating the twenty-first century.

About the Interviews

YTI recruited participants from across the United States and from a wide variety of church groups. During their month on campus, the participants engaged in service learning, took elective classes in theology, took part in small-group reflection, and lived in community with one another. YTI also established a program of research with these young people, in order to learn more about the religious lives of adolescents.

In the early 1990s, as a doctoral student at Emory studying similar issues, I, along with others, helped to design and carry out a program of research that included the life-narrative interviews on which this book is based. The designers of the YTI program initially inherited a framework for research from a sister program, nontheological in focus, that had been the model for YTI's overall plan. This research model focused on the collection of data through various standardized-test measures (such as evidence of increasing critical-thinking capacities, or changes in methods of moral reasoning) that could be analyzed for matters of interest to educators. To that basic research template, we added narrative interviews.

What became immediately clear during the first summer of research with youth was that our inherited testing-based forms of research fit neither the young people in whose lives we were interested nor the framework of values and epistemology that guided the kind of research we wanted to do. Those empirical methods belonged to a different research paradigm, one more interested in tabulating standardized responses of large groups of youth to get at general statements that would be, in some sense, true of all youth. Our team's interest, in contrast, was to glean insights into the religious lives of particular youth from their own in-depth narrations of their stories and ideas. I hated the test-based models of data collection, and so did the youth at YTI. As a result, we soon abandoned test-based methods in favor of a research process completely based on life-narrative interviewing. In the process, we learned that interviews are an especially good method of learning about girls. We also learned that the girls themselves used the interview sessions for purposes of their own—as a chance to step out of their busy activities and think about their lives, as an opportunity to make connections and gather their own insights, and as a chance to speak to an attentive listener about things that really mattered in their lives.

Who Are the Girls?

All the girls were between the ages of sixteen and eighteen at the time of their interviews. They had come from across the country, representing nineteen different states, and they identified themselves as belonging to seventeen different Christian denominations, as follows: African Methodist Episcopal (1), American Baptist (1), Baptist (7), Progressive Baptist (2), Church of the Brethren (1), Christian Missionary Alliance (1), Episcopal (4), Lutheran (1), Methodist (8), three nondenominational Christian churches (6), Pentecostal (2), Presbyterian (6), Roman Catholic (7), United Church of Christ (2), and Unitarian Universalist (1). They came from single-parent families, blended families, so-called traditional nuclear families, and extended-family households. Among this group of girls was a diversity of racial and ethnic heritages; they identified themselves as African American (12), African Caribbean (5), Asian American (4), European American (28), and Middle Eastern (1). Most were from middle-class or upper-middle-class families, with a few (8) from working-class families.[9] I offer this summary in order for readers to have a picture of the diversity represented in the group of girls interviewed for this book, not in order to make any broader generalizations from my research to all adolescent girls. Instead, this type of interview research is an effort to listen closely to the nuances and insights shared by one small group of girls, and to see what may be discovered from them.

EXPLANATION OF TERMS. The interviews used for this book have three features in common: they all involve girls who were Christian adolescents at the time they were interviewed. But this statement may not provide much information, because the terms "adolescence," "girl," and "Christian" all have contested meanings today.

Adolescence. Only a few years ago, the term "adolescence" rather straightforwardly referred to the age span and developmental features of people between twelve and eighteen or nineteen. This designation carried a variety of assumptions about the people it designated, such as the idea that these years constitute a waiting period in between childhood and adulthood, a period characterized by hormonally induced turmoil, stress, and anguish. In the mid-twentieth century, under the influence of such developmental psychological paradigms as that of Erik Erikson, the idea of adolescence as a time of "identity formation" took hold in popular language and consciousness.

These days, scholars and researchers as well as teachers, youth ministers, counselors, and others who work with adolescents note that the age range under consideration has broadened. People now considered to fit within the category of adolescence may be as young as ten and as old as twenty-five or even thirty in some cultural contexts. The period of youth marked by the name "adolescence" is often seen as beginning with the onset of the physical changes of puberty but ending with social markers of entry into the so-called adult world, markers like acquisition of a full-time job, choice of a mate, or acquisition of such property as a car or a home. In other words, the period designated by the term "adolescence" is not fixed but varies according to cultural contexts and the meanings of adulthood.

Moreover, although scholars and practitioners working with youth today note the presence of certain common developmental features among people who are called adolescents, they are far less certain that there exists a single stair-step-like pattern of growth and change that fits all young people. Studies of youth in different cultures suggest that the different meanings and expectations that a particular culture holds for its youth play an important role in shaping what adolescence looks like in that culture. In some cultures, for example, the idea that youth are inherently rebellious or in a period of necessary psychological upheaval simply does not fit. Therefore, it is far more problematic these days to speak of adolescents as a single group unified by a particular set of characteristics.

"Adolescence," then, is not a fixed term with fixed meanings. Rather, it is a concept embodying multiple meanings that are continuously in the process of being sorted out by those who use the term. As I use the term in this book, "adolescence" refers to that time in life that is bracketed on one side by the meanings of childhood and on the other by those of adulthood. This is a helpful way to describe the general period of life in which, despite wide variations, certain commonly experienced changes appear to take place among humans and move them toward adulthood. These changes involve shifts in cognitive abilities, which affect the complexity with which people can think about and act on the world; the development of new physical capacities for performing a variety of tasks (in sports, for example, or in various forms of labor) in addition to sexual and reproductive changes; and new relational capacities that permit new kinds of connections with others. The term "adolescent" refers to a person in the midst of these changes.

"I Am a Girl—Whatever That Means." Just as the term "adolescence" has undergone changes in meaning, such words as "girl," "woman," "boy," and "man," which are used to designate a person's gender, do not hold singular, unchanging meanings. What is a girl? For people in my parents' generation, such a question would have seemed silly: people were either boys or girls, male or female; that determination was based on biological sex characteristics, and the two distinct identities of male and female were understood to be opposites (hence the phrase "the opposite sex"). My parents would have considered a person's identity as either a boy or a girl to be the fixed, given result of biological differences.

Today, however, shifts in understanding among scholars who work to understand gender identity have led to a distinction between the terms "sex" and "gender." On the one hand, biological characteristics that serve as the basis for one's designation as a male or a female refer to one's sex. On the other hand, the social and cultural meanings ascribed to one's designation as a female or a male in a given historical and cultural context are involved in what is called "gender."

Every society sorts out what it considers to be appropriate or natural behavior for men and for women. If we could compare, for several different cultures, lists of appropriate male behavior with lists of behavior considered appropriate for females, we would probably see that some kinds of behavior that are deemed masculine in one culture are considered feminine in another. That is because the terms "appropriate" and "natural," like the terms "sex" and "gender," refer to evaluations that are made, and meanings that are ascribed, on the basis of distinctions that are themselves based on physical sexual characteristics. Such meanings are constructed—shaped by human beings, by their cultures and societies—rather than given or essential in nature. One result of this distinction between sex and gender, then, is the realization that gender is a feature of human experience that societies shape. The *meaning* of being a girl is therefore subject to change. This claim is certainly justified in connection with the group of girls interviewed for this book, whose definitions of the words "girl" and "woman" ranged from "someone capable of bearing a child" and "someone who belongs to the part of humanity who are more imaginative, more connected, more powerful" to "the ones who aren't boys and so are always on the down side of whatever happens."

When it comes to defining girlhood, recent literature on adolescent girls has been just as varied and confusing as the voices of these girls.

After years of silence about girls, researchers began to study young women in schools, juvenile detention facilities, and clinics. Studies from the 1980s and 1990s spoke about girls as being "shortchanged" by educational systems oriented toward the success of boys.[10] They claimed that boys acted out their internal pain in publicly destructive activity, such as vandalism or risky driving, whereas girls became "quietly disturbed," turning their pain in on themselves through self-destructiveness manifested in eating disorders, depression, and self-mutilation.[11]

Studies on the health of girls noted skyrocketing rates of eating disorders among middle-class and affluent white girls in connection with media-promoted images of the ideal of female beauty as a waiflike thinness. Mary Pipher's popular *Reviving Ophelia*[12] and research by Carol Gilligan and her associates[13] spoke of the shift into adolescence as a time in girls' lives that was marked by a loss of self.

A second generation of research on adolescent girls has begun to offer some modifications of this gloomy portrayal of girlhood, suggesting that such variables as race and ethnicity may matter in girls' perceptions of their bodies and beauty. For example, some scholars suggest that African American girls, whose bodies often fall outside the culturally specific norms of beauty heralded by Euro-American-oriented advertising and film, appear to be less subject to the negative power of these cultural portrayals of physical attractiveness.[14] Others note that women and girls, although still experiencing gender-based discrimination in many ways, have made substantial gains in education, work, income, and other arenas in recent decades. Among those pushing hardest to erase the image of girls as particularly oppressed are writers of the emerging literature focused on boys. These writers respond to the attention that has been generated for girls by the girl studies of the past two decades with assertions that boys are the ones who really need the special attention and help of society. The picture they paint of girls and girlhood is therefore fairly rosy.[15]

I suspect that the real story is somewhere in between these two frameworks for thinking about girls. On the one hand, girls have experienced difficulties that are shaped by their living in a society stratified by gender. On the other hand, some gains have been made, at least for some young women. What all of this suggests is that we cannot speak of "girls" or "girlhood" as if these terms possessed a singular meaning, any more than the term "adolescence" does. Used by a marine sergeant or a men's athletic coach, the term "girl" is likely to be an insult: "You all act like a bunch of girls!" or "You're throwing like a girl!" By contrast, the term "girl" as used by a contemporary educator may designate a member of a highly productive, imaginative group of fast learners who solve problems through cooperation. Coming from a young woman herself, the term "girl" may refer, on the surface level, to the sex of the person it designates, but with that designation comes a host of diverse meanings that include distinctions in status and power.

In this book, I use the term "girl" to refer, first, to those young people participating in the Youth Theological Initiative who identified themselves as being of the female sex. But in interview questions I also used the term as a point of inquiry, asking girls about the meanings and associations they attached to this term, and about how they had come to their perspectives on being a girl. I wanted to find out what kinds of characteristics and behavior the young women participating in this research identified with being a girl, and what, if anything, their gender identity might have to do with their religious lives.

On Being a Christian. The last identity term to consider here is "Christian." Literally, of course, this word refers to someone who is a follower or disciple of Christ. The two millennia of Christianity leading up to the present time testify to how many different meanings may be attributed to that simple definition; kinship groups have come to blows and nations have fought wars over such distinctions. And hundreds of denominational groups, all laying claim to the name "Christian" in some way, have been formed on the basis of nuances, small or large, in the meanings of this term.

For this project, I selected interviews with girls who had named themselves as Christians. Nearly all YTI participants do so, although from time to time there have also been youth of other faiths, and even of no faith. As described earlier, among the girls who participated in the research interviews were Christians of many different denominational traditions. This means, at a minimum, that the girls who were my research partners in these interviews, although they were all Christian, had some rather different understandings and practices of Christian faith. To give just one example, a Roman Catholic girl spoke about praying the rosary as a way she practices her faith through prayer; another girl, raised a Southern Baptist, asked, "What's a rosary?"

Nevertheless, these girls had enough common interest in religious and theological matters to spend a month of their summer at an academy focused on such issues. They also had in common the fact that they all had entered adolescence in the United States during the post-Vietnam, post-Watergate rise of evangelical Christianity as a political and cultural force. The latter circumstance meant that these girls' own particular definitions of faith and religiosity inevitably had been formed in some kind of relation to assumptions about religion and its meanings that were mediated by the general culture. As the interviews clearly show, many of the girls had struggled against popular perceptions of what it meant to be a religious person, perceptions that involved meanings of the term "Christian" that were different from their own meanings. Others, by contrast, found that popular culture's understandings of faith—as a guiding set of moral norms, or as a set of stated beliefs to which people give their assent—fit their own understanding of the terms "religious" and "Christian." The interviews, instead of attempting to force particular definitions of Christianity on the interview subjects, invited these girls to explore their perspectives on what it meant in their own lives to be religious and Christian.

Throughout this book, I use the terms "religion," "religious lives," and "spirituality" almost interchangeably. Nevertheless, for many people today, teens and adults alike, the distinctions between and among these words matters a great deal, so I will take a minute to say more about what I mean by each of them.

"Religion" refers to the systems of signs, symbols, rituals, and practices that constitute the worldviews through which people and communities organize their lives in relation to the sacred. That is, religion is a way of making and expressing meaning on the basis of a people's experiences and understandings of transcendence. Religions, although they connect people with that which is extraordinary, mysterious, holy, and sacred, make use of the ordinary, everyday materials and ideas of a particular culture for their expression. The term "religion" also refers to the body of knowledge, or tradition, out of which a people has, over time, shaped its communal beliefs and practices. Thus religion is not merely a matter of individual belief, or of ideas to which a person assents. It is instead a communally situated, shared way of life that includes beliefs, commitments, and practices in the living out of a worldview.

I use the term "religious lives" to draw attention to the religious dimension of girls' lives. This term makes explicit the understanding that there is a religious dimension to the lives of the girls in this study, regardless of whether that religiosity is immediately visible in distinctively religious language or practices. It is not as if adolescent girls separate their days or hours into religious and nonreligious ones; these girls are not like cats with nine lives, one of which is religious while the rest are something else. For these girls, the making of religious meaning may take place in relation to any aspect of life; it is not restricted to ideas or actions with explicitly religious content, such as praying, attending church services, or reading the Bible. Rather, girls go about embodying their religion in everyday life, and in many ways. Common experiences like watching a film, listening to music, or engaging in other forms and activities of popular culture are also examples of practices through which many girls engage in making religious meaning. To speak of the religious lives of girls, then, is to issue an invitation to remember this dimension in the whole of girls' experiences and attend to it explicitly.

"Spirituality" is a word that has come into widespread use in the United States in recent years. I use the term in this book to refer to a person's or a community's intimate awareness of God and to the desire to live a life in relation to God, as expressed in such practices as discernment, prayer, hospitality, and service to others. Spirituality may be understood as an aspect of religion, especially the lived, experienced practices of religion. But for some people, including some of the girls who are the focus of this book, the primary meaning of the term "spirituality" may be found in its distinction from religion. "I'm spiritual but not religious," say a number of these girls. Like many others in our society who make such a statement, these girls mean that they possess a sense of connection with God but take issue with some of what is commonly understood by the term "religious." Later on, I will explore in greater detail such statements by the adolescent girls in the interviews. The main thrust of such comments, however, is the idea that a person can have an awareness of the sacred and can engage in practices that connect him or her with sacredness while also being critical of certain expressions of spirituality within particular religious or denominational traditions.

But spiritualities do not spring forth in a vacuum. They arise out of people's experiences that are rooted in particular cultures and contexts, experiences tacitly and explicitly shaped by the religious perspectives of those cultures and contexts. Although a given individual may well engage in spiritual practices apart from participation in a religious tradition, I think it is overstating the case to assert that something called "spirituality" exists in some mode that is sanitized of the mediating impact of religious worldviews. Against the grain, then, of popular assertions of a spirituality free from religion, I do not use the term "spirituality" to connote opposition to religion (unless, of course, such use reflects a particular girl's intended meaning). Instead, the term "spirituality," in this volume, concerns the living shape of people's and communities' intimate relationships with the sacred. For many of us, spirituality is formed and lived out in faith communities.

A NOTE OF CAUTION. Because my study of the religious lives of girls draws from a particular group of young women, I am not assuming that this collective portrait can be generalized to all adolescent girls. The research project from which this book emerged was not based on efforts to achieve a representative sample through interviews, or to find something resembling a typical or average adolescent girl—as if such a girl existed in real life anyway! Rather, this portrait of adolescent girls looks closely at one particular group, in an effort to add to the growing body of knowledge and understanding about girls that is already available from other kinds of studies. In order to protect the anonymity of the girls who participated in this research, I have changed the names as well as some of the identifying information about each girl. The risk in doing so is that of obliterating a girl's particularity. In this instance, however, I understand my commitment to these girls as one that accepts that risk in order to keep faith with them in terms of their anonymity.

What Lies Ahead

This book offers a portrait of the religious lives of a group of adolescent girls as well as of the family relationships in which their religious lives took shape. It is sketched from the stories of a group of girls who hailed from all across the United States and who came from a diversity of racial, ethnic, class, and denominational backgrounds. Although the chapters that follow place the girls' voices in the foreground, I want to be clear that I do not see myself as giving voice to these girls; these girls already speak for themselves, and with robust and vibrant stories. This book is my interpretation of their stories and remarks, written from the standpoint of my context as an Anglo, North American, middle-class woman, as a feminist theologian and scholar of religion, and as a pastor and practitioner of the Christian faith rooted in the Reformed tradition of Christianity. Like any other context, mine sheds light on certain things while obscuring others, and so it is important for readers to know something about the background that informs my writing. At the same time, however, it is my hope that, through my admittedly partial way of making sense of what the girls talked about in their interviews, the perspectives of the girls who are the subjects of this book can be freshly perceived, and that something about who they are as young women of faith is authentically present in these pages.

GIRL TALK

A WAY OF HEARING THE LIVES OF

ADOLESCENT GIRLS

ELAINE, SEVENTEEN YEARS OLD when she attended the Youth Theological Initiative and participated in its interview research, bounded into the library conference room where the interview was to take place.

"Is this going to take long?" she wanted to know. "We're going out for a Coke in a little while."

An hour and a half later, the time and the outing forgotten, Elaine was immersed in talking with me about her religious beliefs, her family, and what it is like to be a girl in this day and age. Initially unsure that she was "worth interviewing," since she didn't really "know that much," Elaine discovered in the course of the interview that she had a lot to say about all these topics.

She talked about her family situation, complicated by the fact that her parents were getting a divorce, "like right now." She also described the crucial role of her youth minister in helping her cope with the transitions in her family life: "God is always with me and gives me the people I need to get through. So I can trust that everything will be all right in the long run."

At the end of the YTI program, she spoke about her interview experience this way: "At first I thought, 'Oh, research—I don't want to do that.' But then I decided it might be interesting to do the interview, and I just started talking, and before long I was saying things about my life I haven't had time to think about. It was really good. I found out about my life by telling *you* about it."

Finding out by telling—that is a good way to describe what often happens in interviews with adolescent girls. Formal interviews as well as informal conversations with a researcher who listens to them can become opportunities for girls to sort out, and even to construct anew, what they know, think, and feel. In this chapter, while describing the process of listening to girl talk in interviews, I will briefly introduce a few of the girls along with some of the insights and issues concerning their religious lives that inform this book. Sharing these girls' voices helps to situate the book's underlying research, in which fifty girls talked about their religious lives, their families, and being female in interviews lasting about two hours.[1]

Finding Out by Telling

Human beings are "storied" people. That is, we both express and shape our personhood through the stories we tell about ourselves and our world. Contemporary thinkers, following the sociologist Peter Berger, sometimes refer to this as the "social construction of reality." Others, in the tradition of the late French philosopher Michel Foucault, refer to the "productive power of discourse," a phrase that describes the deep connections between the lives we narrate and the events and relationships that take place in our lives. Recent developments in the emerging therapeutic method known as narrative therapy put forth the notion that often disabling problems encountered by people or groups have at their source a "problem" story shaping the limits of who those people can be and how they can act. This kind of therapy consists in helping people deconstruct such harmful narratives and replace them with "preferred narratives," that is, life-enhancing stories. The idea behind this perspective on healing is that how we speak about something has the power to shape our experiences.

When a girl speaks in an interview such as the ones conducted for this project, she engages in the act of constructing a story that comprises a particular version of reality. In telling her story at this particular time and in this place, she shapes new meanings and may find herself offering new interpretations of a story she has told many times to others. Storytelling is most centrally an imaginative act of making meaning, a process of making sense of one's world and experiences, of giving significance to certain relationships and experiences while making little of others. An interview is a moment of self-narration in which a girl creates anew the way she wishes to be known. As she stresses a certain situation, feeling, thought, or relationship, the points of her experience worthy of such "accent marks" begin to comprise a new story, a new way of narrating her life. This new story is not made up, in the sense of being a lie, and yet it is newly made up for this particular hearing. The interview comprises a focused opportunity for a girl to "restory" her life.

Researchers have to make choices about how to engage and honor the particular identities and contexts of research participants, knowing that these are always partial renderings at best. For this book, I did not employ the kind of case study methodology chosen by some contemporary ethnographers as my primary framework for representing in writing my research with girls. It is true that this kind of methodology allows a researcher to flesh out interview subjects' particular backgrounds and contexts in greater detail, but case studies also bind descriptions to a few people, who are then treated as representative.

In contrast to that approach, my research process was grounded in an understanding of interviewing as a relational practice in which encounter elicits insights. Rather than treating these interviews as "eternal," freezing girls in a particular moment in time as if that is who they were and are and always will be, I engaged in what Sarah Lightfoot-Lawrence and Jessica Hoffmann Davis have called "portraiture": taking "snapshots" within a specific time frame and context, from which insights and generative themes can be drawn to provide a way of learning—in this case, learning more about the religious lives of girls.[2] Portraiture offers a partial glimpse of someone situated in time, not a vision of the whole person across all time. Therefore, what we may learn from it is also partial and should not be confused with the whole of a person's life. For that reason, in this book I have adopted the sometimes awkward-sounding practice of using the past tense when sharing what girls said in their interviews, so as not to contribute to the myth that I am presenting the girls themselves, or the myth that what they said at one moment in time equates with who they are now and with what they will be saying forever. And in this research, the technique of portraiture was less focused on any single individual than on a whole group of girls.

But even with careful efforts to define and explain research practices, distortions and problems are inevitable in research conducted by and with human beings. Therefore, a final caveat: remember that this book represents my interpretations. I do this kind of research in the hope of contributing to a larger understanding of the religious lives of adolescent girls, in fresh ways that can also contribute to their well-being. Despite the potential problems and limitations of interviews, I still value ethnographic interview methods as a way of learning from and about interview subjects. In this case, my interviews became a way of hearing about the faith lives of adolescent girls—not the only way, but surely a valuable and important one.

The Religious Lives of Adolescent Girls: Snapshots

When girls at YTI talked about their lives and their religious faiths, they often wove together stories of activities, ideas, and relationships—activities worth doing, ideas worth thinking about and believing in, and people worth knowing. Mixed in with mundane descriptions of having "too much homework," or of there being "nothing to do around here," girls shaped narratives about, for example, a parent's illness causing them to work hard to answer questions about why a good and loving God allows human suffering. Among humorous tales of pranks played on teachers, girls also spun stories that showed them wrestling with models of adulthood, of female gender identity, and of living out the integrity of their core beliefs in their relationships. These narratives of girls' everyday lives, and of their struggles to make sense of the "big questions" posed within everyday encounters, comprise girl talk on faith.

What are some of the ways these girls described themselves and their religious lives? Two snapshots of individual girls, chosen as interesting examples of the connections among religion, gender, and family relationships, will begin to introduce this group of girls and their perspectives. These two examples clearly show the importance these girls attached to defining religion in their own terms, apart from the received definitions that were common in their immediate worlds. They also convey the way everyday relationships with parents, pastors, and peers comprise the stuff of religious reflection and of girls' efforts to make meaning. These snapshots illustrate the way girls' lives of faith have to do simultaneously with what is most personal and individual and with their deep desire to participate in events and causes bigger than themselves alone. And, finally, these snapshots convey the importance girls attached to living lives of integrity—that is, living in such a way that their actions and outwardly visible selves were consonant with the viewpoints, values, and principles of their articulated convictions.

Kendra: "My Religion Is Who I Am"

Kendra, describing an average day in her life, spoke of days filled with activity: time spent "just hanging out" with friends before school, hours passed in classrooms that were "mostly boring, with a few brief exceptions," and after-school basketball practices. Once home from school, she had a routine of homework and chores, practicing the piano, and checking in with her parents as well as a lot of time spent listening to music or talking with friends on the telephone.

"What elements of such a day would you consider part of your religious life, or connected to your faith?" I asked her in an interview.

"All of it," she replied. "It's all part of my faith. I mean, my religion is who I am. It's not like a piece of clothing I put on and take off. It's me, so it's in everything I do and say."

Kendra's sense of the entire fabric of her life as faith-connected contrasted significantly with what she believed other young people from her hometown meant when they spoke of being "religious." Many of her peers at school, for instance, held that Christians had to engage in certain activities, such as specific forms of prayer or a discipline of daily Bible reading, to qualify as Christians under the terms defined by their social context. Unlike these peers, Kendra said, "I don't have any rituals."

> I don't. I mean, everybody always tells me if you just read your Bible every night, you'll feel so much better. Read your Bible every night, read your Bible every morning, read your Bible once a day, get up early and read it, get up early and pray. And I know it's important, and I do it for a while, and then I start feeling guilty. I'll quit for a day, and then I'll get off the bandwagon, and I'll feel so guilty. And I don't . . . so rituals have kind of done me more harm than good.

For Kendra, an important question at the time of her interview concerned whether observing a daily quiet time—or any other particular set practice, for that matter—defined a person as a Christian. What, for Kendra, defined faith? What did she believe that was like the beliefs of others around her? In what ways was her religious self-understanding different from that of her parents, her peer group, or her community?

Kendra's family situation was difficult; her mother suffered from a long-term chronic and debilitating illness. In her interview, Kendra spoke of earlier times when she had blamed or resented her mother for being so sick. Then she had gone on to blame God. In the previous few years, however, she had gained a new perspective on the matter of God and her mother's illness.

"I know it's not her fault," she said. "But I always used to ask why God would let this happen to her. Now I try to think about why God, who is good, can stand to have such awful things go on."

For Kendra, reflections on the story of Jesus' passion on the cross provided new ways of thinking about how God has empathy.

"God knows about watching someone you love suffer. I don't understand it all, but at least it helps me think that God understands how I feel."

Defining faith, sorting out what kinds of faith practices really matter, God's relationship to pain and suffering in the world—these are some of the issues Kendra wrestled with during her time at YTI, and in her interview. For Kendra, everyday life provided the raw material for constructing a faith perspective. Not content to accept popular definitions of faith, or the unexamined assumptions about God offered by peers and the surrounding culture in which she lived, Kendra was deeply engaged in the hard work of making religious meaning. Clearly, anyone who wanted to know this adolescent girl at a level deeper than superficial generalities would need to know about her religious life.

Kelly: Imagining a World Governed by the Golden Rule

Kelly was a lively, outspoken girl who at the time of her interview was headed toward her senior year in an all-girls' Catholic high school, although neither she nor any members of her family were Catholic.

"I go there for the good education," she explained, "and also because it's all girls, which is supposed to give you more opportunities if you are a girl, and I think it does. See," she explained further, animated in gestures and tone, "I've always gone to a girls' school. So to me, I've never really had the competition. I can't even think about not being picked for a job or anything because I was a woman. I've always had woman teachers, and, you know, that's just the way it's always been. I love it. I'm sending my daughter to a girls' school, I don't care what she says! I love it."

She resented the fact that in this environment of strong women, a male priest was required for leadership of the weekly Eucharist service at the school.

"I'm Unitarian Universalist," she reminded me. "We try not to tell other people what to believe."

When I asked Kelly to talk about her understanding of God, and about how she lived her religion in her everyday life, she tended to talk about people. She described in detail her close relationship with one of her teachers, an eighty-year-old nun, with whom she became especially close after sharing feelings about the death of her grandfather. Her family life had been complicated by her parents' divorce and by some lingering sadness from childhood, but she spoke of having "decent" relationships with both parents at the time of her interview, even though her relationship with her father had been severely strained.

In addition to her mother, whom she described as "the most giving person on the planet," Kelly easily identified several adults from her church and at school who were important in shaping her religious life. Among these important adults were this nun, who taught at her school and with whom she had become quite close, and her youth minister. She credited these relationships with helping her develop her particular understanding of Christianity, a perspective on faith as "more about what you do than what you think, and even more about how you treat other people."

Kelly intended to live her faith in various efforts aimed at "making the world a better place, not just for people but for all God's creatures." Even before coming to YTI and participating in its programs of service learning, Kelly had engaged in several different types of volunteer work to help others. She had also participated in her church's active protests against legislation pitting the interests of businesses against the environment, and in her church's activities in support of access to health care and affordable housing for those who are poor. Kelly's perspectives on faith put relationships and fair, caring treatment of others at the center of her thoughts and actions.

"I love my church. It was, like, really instrumental in the civil rights movement, so I'm really proud of it. . . . I love it because I love the people. Unitarianism's definition is that its just a religion that you don't have to hold to any creed to belong to as long as you respect other people's spirituality and are kind and fair to the people around you, and you really live by the Golden Rule. That would be the number one thing I cherish."

The issue of respect for the beliefs of others, she told me, was precisely what had led up to a major misunderstanding about her faith by some of the members of her church. Kelly described her congregation as being full of "regular people and also ex-hippies," an activist kind of place, so that when issues of injustice arose, the church often would take to the streets in protest and advocacy. On one such occasion, members of the church created a banner, with the church's name on it, bearing a slogan signaling support for a woman's right to terminate a pregnancy by having an abortion. Recalling that experience, Kelly spoke at length about her personal beliefs:

> I had a really bad experience last year. You see, I'm pro-life because I was born when I was only six months in the womb. And I stayed in an incubator for a long time. I was in intensive care for a long time. But the point is, I lived, I'm here. But in my state you can have an abortion that late, and I'm like, "No, those are babies that are like me—I'm

sorry." And so then the whole church made a big banner announcing
COMMUNITY UNITARIAN UNIVERSALIST CHURCH: PRO-CHOICE. I was
obviously upset. I really believed my beliefs should be respected in that
way, because the only belief our church holds in common is to be
respectful of other persons' beliefs. And they went and marched around
with it.

She arranged with her youth pastor to preach a sermon the following
Sunday in which she called people back to this most central belief in
respect for others.

Missing from this portrait of an adolescent girl's religious life is any
linear formula that easily lines up particular religious beliefs with a set
political ideology. At the time of this interview, Kelly was, in her words,
a "pro-life feminist," a Unitarian who had come, through the caring ministry of a Roman Catholic sister, to imagine Jesus as "God in human
form"; before that, she said, she hadn't really believed much in God.

"What would the world be like if we all lived by the Golden Rule?"
she asked rhetorically. "People would probably still have different ideas
and beliefs. But they'd also have respect. They wouldn't be forcing their
ways on each other."

In this brief snapshot of Kelly, we see a young woman's quest to live
her beliefs with authenticity, and in a way that calls those around her to
do the same. Kelly's exposure to some form of religious education displays itself in her easy use of explicitly Christian religious language, such
as in her allusions to the Golden Rule, God in human form, and even her
brief reference to all God's creatures. This is a portrait of a young woman
whose view of the world has been shaped in significant ways by her education and immersion in Christian religious perspectives, practices, and
language.

At the same time, however, this snapshot does not portray a casual,
unquestioning adoption of religious views handed down from one generation to the next. Rather, in Kelly's narration we see a young woman who
actively wrestles with the meanings and implications of her religious tradition, using the beliefs and language of that tradition to call others (particularly the adults in her faith community) to account for what she
perceives as the gap between their actions and their professed beliefs. For
example, she makes use of the time-honored Roman Catholic practice of
separate education for girls and boys as an arena for discovering and
affirming the power of young women to think, know, and act. As Kelly's
comments illustrate, the religious lives of adolescent girls—even girls participating in churches and faith communities—are not as passive and

compliant as some social science researchers would assert. Instead, Kelly provides an example of how a girl's spirituality can involve her in active wrestling with her faith tradition and in the connections between ideas and actions, a process of struggling to construct beliefs and a way of life that make sense, and that can make a difference beyond herself alone.

Listening as a Contemplative Spirituality of Parenting

One of the best ways to learn about the spiritual lives of adolescent girls is to ask them—and then to listen, carefully and attentively, to the variety of ways in which girls talk about their religious lives. Interviews such as those from which I drew the perspectives of Kendra and Kelly are formal listening opportunities in which there is benefit for both the speaker and the listener. In formal interviews, researchers like me gain insights into the topics and lives of the people we study. But interviewing is not a one-way street. Girls also actively use such interviews for their own purposes. Sometimes people do not know what they think or how they feel about something until they talk about it. Over and over in these interviews, I watched girls figure out what they thought by telling me. This suggests to me that adults, by listening carefully to girls, can participate in helping them sort out what their perspectives, feelings, and experiences mean to them.

Another important aspect of the YTI interviews is that they provided the girls a space in which an adult took time to attend to them. Girls frequently commented at the conclusion of their interviews that no one before had ever listened to them for so much time, or in such a focused way. After all, not even psychotherapy offers a two-hour uninterrupted opportunity for a girl to narrate her life story! Elsewhere, my colleague Dori Grinenko Baker and I have referred to this as an act of "holy listening."[3] When I listen to girls in the careful way that interviews require, I often want to take off my shoes, aware of being on holy ground, because frequently there is a sense that something powerful is taking place in the sharing.

But what does interviewing have to do with the desires of parents and other caring adults to support the religious lives of adolescent girls? Admittedly, this kind of interview offers a somewhat rarified opportunity for listening to an adolescent girl. Parents, naturally, like most other adults whose lives touch those of girls, will not be in situations where they can listen the way an interviewer can. But the process of interviewing does offer some clues about parenting practices that support the religious lives of daughters.

The process of attentive listening suggests that listening itself is so vital, so important to how these girls shape their spiritual lives, that we must find and create multiple opportunities in everyday life to listen to girls if we want to support their spiritual lives. In the kind of interview I am describing here, an adult sits down with a girl, stops every other activity, and attends to her without critique or judgment, for the sole purpose of hearing her. In everyday parent-teen interactions, no one gets two hours of sit-down time. But often people do get ten minutes in the car on the way to a game, or a few moments in the kitchen while preparing a snack, or a quick conversation on the way out the door, the kind of interaction that usually gets filled up with the logistics of where a daughter is going and who else will be there. Taking such moments as chances to practice holy listening offers parents many small opportunities to hear the lives of adolescent daughters and may open the way for somewhat longer times, when parents can hear more than just quick reflections from girls.

The practice of holy listening that I am talking about here is actually rooted in ancient practices of contemplative prayer in the Christian tradition, practices in which people strive to empty themselves of agendas, worries, and even words. The reason for bracketing off one's own agendas and noisiness in the act of contemplative prayer is simple: doing so creates an opening, a space where God might be encountered. And contemplative listening, or holy listening, is a way of attending to another person on the basis of the same dynamics as those found in contemplative prayer. In contemplative forms of prayer, the focus is less on *talking to* God and more on *listening for* God. Similarly, in contemplative, or holy, listening, we bracket off our inner noisiness and even our actual speaking in order to make space for another—our teenage daughter—to give voice to her life, her thoughts, her feelings. Ours is an intentional act of being as fully present to and for another as is humanly possible.

When my children were younger, opportunities for contemplative listening often came around bedtime as we went through the nightly rituals of reading stories, saying prayers, singing lullabies, and settling into bed. At those times, younger children often become reflective about the day when they sense that adults are listening. I thought of such moments as little windows of openness into the soul, when my children felt connected to me and openly shared what had been of greatest importance and urgency during the day, and when I could be with them in a special way.

With teens, we are no longer doing this kind of parenting work, putting them to bed with lullabies and stories. Far too often, they are still awake, on the phone or listening to music, long after exhaustion and sleep have overtaken us. And other factors may complicate opportunities for close sharing at other times as young women emotionally push for more space in relationships with family members or actively renegotiate the forms of engagement they desire with their parents as they move toward young adulthood. But the basic need to be acknowledged and blessed by parents nevertheless remains during adolescence, even though it may require different forms of expression than during the childhood years.

One friend, the parent of a fifteen-year-old girl, told of converting the story time of earlier years with her daughter to a nightly check-in ritual.

"I don't go into her room to say bedtime prayers anymore, obviously," she laughed. "What we do now came into being gradually. As she got older, I started checking in at bedtime, stopping by her room and asking if she's okay and ready to tuck in for the night. Sometime in there I started saying, 'Is there anything keeping you from putting the day to rest?' She'd tell me if there was something bothering her, or if she was too excited about something to go to sleep, and so we'd talk for a little. I got a chance to listen to her apart from the busy-ness of the day. Now it's more of a shorthand. I say, 'Putting the day to rest?' And she'll talk a little. If I'm headed to bed first, she'll say it to me. It's a little ritual we do just to touch base. And we can do it even when we're mad at each other!"

Windows for contemplative listening with girls may open up around elation or disappointment over academic or athletic performance, if adults can set aside their own reactions, commentaries, and feelings about the poor grade, or the record performance at the swim meet, long enough to really hear how a girl talks about her experience. Setting adult needs aside, or at least temporarily suspending them (the need, for example, to clarify what our house rules are regarding visitors when parents are not home), can invite a listening space in which a girl can express what is most important to her about her friends, or how she prefers to spend time with them, or perhaps even some of the hurt and disappointment she has gone through in friendships.

The process of listening to girls in interviews suggests yet another clue about how parents can support the faith lives of their daughters. These interviews also reveal the importance of other adult listeners who stand alongside listening parents to care for the spiritual lives of girls. Parents have an important and unique role with their own children, but sometimes, as girls rework their relationships with their mothers and fathers, there are points when it is difficult for them to tell their "heart stories" to their parents. At such times, many girls welcome the chance for a friend's parent to listen attentively to them. Caring for the spiritual lives of their own daughters calls parents into practices of care and concern for other people's adolescent daughters as well.

There were a number of such adults in my own adolescence: parents of friends, music teachers, a pastor; people who listened with intentionality and focus. When I could not imagine my own mother holding my beliefs in high esteem—after all, how profound could my thoughts be, when I couldn't even seem to remember to feed the dog every day?—I found that the mother of one of my friends listened to me as if I were incredibly interesting, as if what I had to say really was important. And I believe now, as I did when I was fourteen, that she actually did give importance to what I had to say. Such communally situated practices of listening continue to be crucial to the lives of girls today.

Thus a primary way we can support the spiritual well-being of our own girls is through a kind of shared parenting in which we have a stake in the lives of other girls as well. This is a call to recover the rich meanings of *godparenting,* which went far beyond the symbolic act of standing beside a godchild's parents at the baptismal font. Godparenting at an earlier time in Christian tradition entailed a relationship in which the godparents pledged their presence, care, and resources to support someone else's child. In this day and age, all our children, but especially adolescent daughters, need other adults who can godparent them along the journey of adolescence. As one father I know put it, "Kayla doesn't necessarily talk to me about her inner world. I don't always know directly from her what matters most to her. But I try to talk with her friends, to be another adult they can relate to. And every once in a while Kayla joins in, and I can listen to her, too."

Not all interactions with a daughter can or should be moments of contemplative listening: parents still need to find out when her soccer practice will happen, and how she will get home from Julie's house after school; the garbage still has to go out, and the huge cell phone bill that just came really has to be discussed. I am not naively suggesting that every parental conversation with an adolescent girl can miraculously turn into a deep encounter. Instead, I am saying that, as these interviews with girls suggest, the act of being listened to is so important to girls that parents who want to support their daughters' spiritual lives must retool themselves to listen contemplatively at least some of the time.

Reflections

In concluding this chapter, I am aware of a sense of gratitude for the listeners in my own life, those people who formally and informally have crafted spaces of holy listening and deep attentiveness across the years. Ultimately, the act of listening to another is a spiritual practice. It embodies a contemplative moment in which the listener momentarily brackets off his or her own noisiness to open a space for encounter with another. Christians believe that in such spaces of encounter we may also encounter God (see Matthew 18:20; Luke 24:13–35).

You may also find it helpful, as a way of relating to the situations of adolescent girls, to recall people in your life whose listening presence upheld, challenged, or honored you in some way. In the next chapter, we turn to listen in on more girl talk, this time exploring, in a more focused thematic form, the variety of ways in which these girls narrated the meanings of religion and faith in their lives.

I asked the girls I spoke with to prepare for their interviews by engaging in some reflection on their lives ahead of time that would help them get ready to tell their stories. So, prior to their interviews, each of the girls completed a life-review exercise, designed by James W. Fowler, called "A Tapestry of My Life."[4] This life-review process helped the girls prepare to share their narratives aloud in a one-to-one interview.

As a researcher, and now as a writer, I too have found it useful to engage in some reflective preparation; thinking about my own adolescent years and reflecting on my life in the present help me to be clearer about the similarities and differences between my own life and the lives of the girls who talked with me. Reviewing my own story of adolescence helps me empathically remember how deeply young women often feel their experiences, how important it can be for them to take action in the world, and how much more thoughtful many youth are than adults credit them with being. Sharing a bit of my own story of being a teenager, as I did in the introduction to this book, reminded me of the special vulnerability experienced by some young women when they narrate their lives. This kind of reflective preparation assists me in my efforts to be open to the stories shared by girls. It helps me to recognize the incredible gift given to me when a girl tells me how she knows God, or why she hurts so much, or what her passionate commitments lead her to do at this time in her life. Each story is indeed a gift.

With that in mind, some readers may also find it valuable to do a little preparation for hearing the stories of the girls in this book. The life-review exercise in the Appendix is one way to do that. You may wish first to complete that exercise as an overall life review and then focus your attention on your teen years, recalling the marker events, people, world events, and images of God that gave that time of life its particular contours. Some people like to remember in the quiet of their own reflections; others find it helpful to share the stories of their teen years. Whichever approach you choose, I hope your reflections will enrich your encounter with the girls in this book, and with the girls in your life.

GIRL TALK ON FAITH

JULIE WAS BORN IN CENTRAL AMERICA, the daughter of American missionaries who worked on behalf of a nondenominational, charismatic Christian organization. She spoke about her faith as someone who had spent her whole life deeply immersed in this particular religious worldview, using words like "sin" and talking easily and freely, in ordinary speech, about "salvation through the cross of Jesus" and about God having a plan for her life. She struggled to explain with clarity exactly how it was that Jesus' dying on the cross worked to save her, but she still described with certainty her conviction that

> the symbol of the cross is really important to me. Just because it reminds me what has been done for me, you know, and maybe what I owe to God . . . it says, like, in the Bible, we should carry our crosses. And that always reminds me when I see it that God gave so much for me, that I owe God, but it also should be a pleasure for me to give. Because that's why I'm here, once again, or it should be why I'm here.

Julie's language seems like fairly conventional, evangelical Christian God talk. She struck me as the sort of young woman who would be identified by peers in high school as "really religious." And yet, asked whether she considered herself to be a religious person, Julie responded vehemently:

> Oh no! No way! I don't consider myself to be religious, because religion has negative connotations to it. When I think of religion, I think of the Renaissance or the Middle Ages and the oppressive Catholic Church. That's just the image I have, and, you know, the defiant denominations that came about in the Reformation. That's what I think about when I think of religion, and the religious wars. And I don't think that's what God is all about. I think that religion is

tradition. And I think that actual spirituality is what I've accomplished in a *relationship* [with God]. I don't consider myself religious. I think spirituality is more personal and is who God is. I don't think God is religion. Humans have created religion as an institution. But I don't think God is an institution. I think He's[1] one being who has a spirit and, you know, I believe in the Trinity. So I think that's where my spirituality comes from, because I have a spirit.

At this point in the interview we both paused, letting that idea soak in for a minute before I sought to further clarify her meaning with a question:

> *Is that where your spirituality comes from? Do you mean it's because you have a spirit and God has a spirit?*
>
> No. What I'm trying to say is that I have *God's* Spirit.

Julie's way of engaging in God talk was steeped in the thought world of the Pentecostal faith in which she had been raised, with its emphasis on believers being filled with God's Spirit. And yet the very same words came out of the mouth of another young woman, whose upbringing and faith perspective were quite different from Julie's. Liza, a sixteen-year-old self-described liberal Episcopalian, spoke with me about experiencing closeness to God in nature, where

> all the electronic noises disappear long enough for me to be aware that I have God's Spirit in me. I belong to God, and there is a little bit of God's light, God's Spirit, that shines through in me. It goes deeper than just repeating the words in the Prayerbook, deeper than religious forms that go through the motions but can't contain the Spirit of God.

Unlike Julie, Liza probably would not be comfortable speaking about Jesus as her personal Lord and savior. And Julie might not even recognize Liza's mention of the "Prayerbook" as referring to the Episcopal Book of Common Prayer, the soul and compass of Episcopalian worship life. Yet both girls spoke of having God's Spirit in them. This form of God talk was, for each of them, a means of expressing the differences between religion as a reflective, authentically lived phenomenon and religion as an empty set of outward forms. Julie and Liza, standing in radically different locations theologically and politically, nevertheless held in common an important concern about faith. Both girls craved authenticity. They each rejected practices of religion that seemed to be merely ritualistic, meaningless processes of going through the motions.

The hunger for authenticity in faith was not the only common thread among the girls I interviewed. These girls—liberal and conservative, evangelical, Catholic, and mainline Protestant, Pentecostals and Presbyterians, members of the African Methodist Episcopal Zion Church and of the Church of the Brethren, Unitarian Universalists, Southern Baptists, and members of many other Christian religious communions—generally rejected a narrow understanding of Christian faith as a mere set of moral strictures. Most did talk about God and faith in personal terms that included individual morality, but they also found diverse ways to express a sense in which faith was more than an individual matter to them, involving public and communal issues as well. Their concerns and actions in relation to matters of racial justice, care for the earth, war, the ethical treatment of animals, affordable housing, how to live well in community with others, and the eradication of poverty were also key dimensions of girl talk on faith.

Given their diverse Christian faith backgrounds, there was no singular form of girl talk on faith among them, but they had much in common with respect to how they experienced and talked about their religious lives. In their interviews, the girls invariably revealed themselves to be thoughtfully and passionately engaged in making sense of their lives, their worlds, and their faith. Accordingly, these girls did not see their faith communities simply as wholesome places where young people could avoid getting into trouble (a perspective on the role of churches often expressed in youth ministry literature, or by parents). Although these girls openly critiqued the church and so-called organized religion, for many of them churches still were places where they sought to work out new understandings of what they believed, and to practice those beliefs in the company of others. In short, the emerging portrait of this group, like their discourse on faith, shows them to be adolescent girls who were concerned about cultivating relationships of care, mutuality, and compassion, who were struggling to live with integrity or coherence between their emerging beliefs and their actions, who were searching for and honoring a sense of purpose or vocation, and who were striving to live justly in a morally complex world.

Embracing a God of Relationships and Love

When girls anywhere talk about God, they use the language and metaphors of their times and cultures. The girls in these interviews were no exception. They spoke of God in parental images, as an "all-loving father," or as "showing unconditional love like my mother tries to, only

God can actually do it." Such metaphors are commonly evoked in American contexts, both religious and secular, as a means of speaking about God. Girls also spoke of God with metaphors of awe, strength, and power: "God is so brilliant that He created a universe where everything works together and fits together somehow." "God is like a giant wind storm, like really big and powerful, but you can't exactly see it." And for many girls, images of friendship were the primary ways of speaking of God: "God? He's my best friend, the one who is always there for me, no matter what."

Relational images of God occurred frequently in these interviews, regardless of whether the girls felt that they possessed or lacked a connection with the God they sought to describe through such images. Sarah, for example, spoke about changes in her uncertain sense of connection with God. She was attending a Catholic high school where she took a variety of religion courses. In one class, "Faith and Ethics," Sarah recalled,

> we just kind of experimented with different types of prayer, as a way to communicate with God. And I had always had classes where we talked *about* God, but I never had classes where we were taught how to talk *to* God. And so that was really weird. You know, I had prayed before, but it was never really sincere. I never felt close to God. It was always like, well, He's out there somewhere. Or He's someone everyone talks about. You know, it was never really a personal relationship. I still don't feel like I have a great personal relationship with God. I don't know if He'll ever talk to me. But I want to have that. And so I think that I'll continue to pray.

In the United States, talk about having a "personal relationship with God" is common in the conservative Protestant subculture of evangelical and some mainline youth ministry programs, and it showed up with considerable frequency in the speech of these girls. To speak of having a personal relationship with God is to make a shorthand reference both to the idea that each person needs to appropriate faith for herself or himself and to the theological notion—not universally held, but certainly common enough in popular discourse—that God loves and relates to each human being personally. Girls using this language seemed to be saying in part that God was not simply an abstract idea for them. God was someone they related to in a profoundly personal way. When the connection with God lacked the intensity or fullness they experienced and yearned for in relationships with friends, family members, boyfriends, and others, some girls expressed a sense of emptiness, loss, and yearning for what was missing.

In Sarah's case, the desire for a personal relationship with God continued to be something for which she prayed. Ironically, this prayer for a closer personal relationship with God led her to other, nonpersonal ways of experiencing the Holy:

> I think I have a greater faith. I feel like I can see God in other people, every day, in everyone. And I feel like sometimes, in a beautiful sunset or something like that . . . maybe God isn't necessarily a personality. Maybe He's more, like, God is love. Like that feeling. Or God is life, or something like that.

Julie referred to God as a "friend," an understanding she placed within the context of God as Creator and as the reason for her being:

> To me, God is why I'm here. I think sometimes people see God as something that was created for *them,* to solve their problems. But I think in actuality God created me because He loved me, and also because He wanted to glorify Himself. That's, to me, why I'm here, not to glorify Him, meaning that I have to do *everything*—like, I have to be right, and that glorifies God. But just knowing Him and getting to know Him, I think that's the most important thing. I think a relationship with God is like any other friendship I have with my friends. It should be—I mean, granted, I can't, you know, sit in my house all day and, you know, just talk to God. It's kind of hard to talk to God throughout the day, I mean. But I think it should be like any other relationship, where you feel open to share anything with them and spend time with them. I think that's how I see God as a friend.

As mentioned, many of the girls described God's characteristics with parental metaphors, saying that to them God was "like a father" or "like a mother." Some girls, however, went so far as to claim that their sense of God was grounded in their relating to a god who was like *their own* fathers or mothers. Dominique, for example, initially struggled with how to characterize God:

> I know some people think of God as like a best friend, like God my father, my daddy. To me, God is like—I don't know, I can't explain Him—just a presence, a powerful being around me that surrounds me and everything I do, and surrounds everybody. I think I'm limiting God's power by saying He's like a friend to me, He's like a father to me, because that's anthropomorphic[2] right there, you know. But [the main person who resembles what God is like] is probably my mom, 'cause she's there for me, and God's always there. My mom is there, the center of my life.

It is striking to hear such claims, when parents so often complain about feeling that they are no longer important in the lives of their teenage daughters.

Seeking Words to Express Mystery

Unlike those girls who primarily used the language of relationships in their God talk, Susan had no interest in using personal language to speak of God. Instead, she actively sought a greater level of abstraction:

> My image of God is kind of an abstract one. God is abstract, and I don't like the whole Father thing, because God is not like a father. At least *my* father is not like a god—I mean, he's my dad. God is like a security blanket. God is like the meditation that you do in yoga, and the sense of peacefulness and, like, sereneness and everything. It's like when we were meditating. It's not like I felt God at that time. It was in the middle of class, and it was early in the morning. But, like, you felt light, and you felt at peace. And then it just kind of let your mind relax, and you could organize yourself so that the problems that you have would be laid out and typed out clearly in your head, and they're not jumbled and you have to search for it. And that's all it was. Um, and it's just this new image I have just come up with recently, and it's very nice and it's very easy to understand. Because this kind of abstract is good for me, because it's a security blanket thing. It's a very big thing for me. It's like, you know, I'm feeling cold, and it, like, warms me up, or like all that kind of good stuff. I've been trying to form an abstract image of God for a very long time.

Kathy also refuted personalistic, human-oriented ways of talking about God, in favor of a more abstract concept:

> God is God and not a woman, not a man. It's a being, a state of mind. It's a different parallel that doesn't exist in the human form.
>
> *So when you think about God, what kind of images do you use?*
>
> Clouds. More around spirituality. A phantasm, not a person.
>
> *What is God like, then?*
>
> For me? Inspirational. Quiet. Reflective. Loving.

Developmental psychologists describe late adolescence as a time when the capacities for abstract and critical thinking can fully emerge so that young people become capable of new, more complex forms of thought.

Susan was actively searching for some more complex ways of thinking about God. On the one hand, she used a familiar and rather concrete illustration ("a security blanket") to name some of the meanings she attached to God. On the other hand, through images of meditation and the workings of the mind, she sought to frame a more abstract way of speaking about God than the limitations of human personalistic terms such as "father" could allow. Susan clearly desired a sense of connection with God, but she needed language that could express this connection without erasing God's *mystery.*

The ability to think about God in more complex, abstract terms brought some girls to a difficult place of wondering if God was merely a creation of their own thoughts. As one girl framed the issue, "If I can talk about my mental image of God in any way I want to, does that mean that God is really only an image, nothing more than the product of my thinking? Does God even exist? I used to have a very clear image of God. Now I'm not so sure, and it's kind of upsetting." Alyssa, for example, spoke of being unsettled by the recognition that her perspectives on God had changed over time:

> Before, I think I just kind of assumed God was just this father image, sort of. You know, real nurturing and wise and kind, and looking down with these nice little crinkly blue eyes and just going, "Hey!" And, um, I don't know, now I see—I see God as—I never really saw him as *active,* you know. He was just something you knew who was there. You weren't required to think about it except at Sunday school. And now I find myself spending a great deal of time contemplating it, and . . . um, I . . . I . . . I vacillate back and forth, between being just completely and solidly convinced that He exists and He is active in everybody's life, too, and wondering if God even exists. Okay, well, I think He *exists.* I'm not sure how *active* He is, though. So I'm asking myself, does He really exist, you know? I guess it just my moods, and it's kind of—I don't know, I'm pretty sure of my faith in it, but—I just think of Him now more as this, well—He doesn't really have that face anymore, I guess. He's just kind of there.

Alyssa's faltering speech underscore the newness of these ideas and her uncertainty about their implications. Several other girls shared this questioning, doubting stance, made most concrete as they began to explore how they no longer thought of God as they had in childhood.

Some girls were obviously unsettled by new images of God, but many appeared to be comfortable with the recognition that their images of God had changed across their lives, even as some of them asserted, as Kit did,

"God Himself is unchanging. It's *my way of thinking about God* that is different." Several girls, comparing their current perspectives on God with those they had held in childhood, spoke of having once pictured God as looking like Santa Claus, or like the old man with the long white beard they associated with Sunday school art.

Kim used a somewhat different image, drawn from cartoons:

> When I was young, I wasn't really sure. I knew, like, God was there. I kind of pictured Him like Casper the Friendly Ghost. You know, He was this nice God standing up there in heaven that told nice stories, and we got to color and do little crafts. It was nice that He was there, but, you know, really—but up until fifth grade, God was there, but I didn't take it to heart. Like when I said that thing about going in my room and asking God into my heart, it was just, like, He had told all these wonderful things, and I wanted all these wonderful things to happen to me. I really didn't think about—you know, I prayed the "Now I lay me down to sleep" thing, but I didn't really take any meaning to it. . . . Now I've got this new image of God. I just picture Him as a quilt. You know, if people make this quilt, like each part is a separate part of their lives. I just picture God as a big quilt, where He has a piece of just everyone in His quilt. And He's not just one color, not like a certain shape. He's the thread that holds them all together.

There was something remarkable going on in the God talk of many of these girls. Many of their images appeared fairly conventional, not deviating much from those commonly found in popular religious language in the United States, images like God as a father, or God as unconditional love. But these girls were also actively creating alternative ways of imagining God. For the girls as a group, religious life had more do to with relationships than with rules. It had to do with how they situated themselves in relation to the sense of vastness and mystery that is God. Their desire for connection and communion with God trumped moralistic notions of God, not because there was no place for ethics in their religious discourse but because religious life, for these girls, consisted principally of a relationship with God that fanned out into connections with family, friends, neighbors, the community, and the wider creation.[3]

The Risks Involved

The sense that they should not ask questions about religious matters formed the unspoken subtext of several of these girls' verbal explorations of a new way of thinking, or of raising questions about received religious teachings. None of the girls who were my partners in these interviews struck me as foolish risk takers, but some were willing to step out on a limb and try on a new perspective. The opportunity in late adolescence for rethinking, questioning, and expanding their understandings of God, welcomed by many girls, came with an element of risk for others. They were strategic in their risk taking, however, exercising a sense of timing and attention to context in deciding when or where or with whom to take risks. One problem they named was that they did not necessarily have adults with whom they felt safe talking about these explorations. And a critical risk, named or hinted at by girls who were moving outside the given bounds of how their families, faith communities, or peer groups thought about God, was the possibility of losing relationships.

Some girls expressed anxiety over the possibility that their parents might reject them for holding religious views or practices that differed from those of their parents. Deana, for example, still participated in the Pentecostal church in which her mother was active. At the age of twelve, she had generally accepted the beliefs and practices of the church, but now her views were changing:

> They believe in not wearing jewelry or pants, for girls, or going to the movies. And when I was twelve, I didn't really care, you know, because I was still a little girl. But then, when I was fourteen, and all my friends were going to the movies or meeting at this certain place, and all I could wear was a skirt and no earrings, I felt, like, out of place. And I started to question, like, why? What does what I wear have to do with my relationship with God? So, um, first I started doing it behind my mother's back. But then after a while I just told her, "I don't want any part of that church anymore." And that hurt her, 'cause my mother was a Sunday school teacher. And she's, like, in charge of the young people's group also. So that really hurt her. Um, I mean, then it became a decision of, should I not hurt her and just stay in it, or should I think about myself?

Girls displayed considerable strategic skill, however, in discerning how and when to diverge from theological perspectives held by family members, or from official church positions. In some situations, for example, they knew that official statements on the status of women were more malleable than in other situations, and they learned to adapt their behavior accordingly. Kendra, for example, learned early from her mother that her school, which she described as "fundamentalist Christian," was not the place to voice ideas about God and gender, women's leadership, and equality:

[At YTI] I've heard stuff that I've never heard before. . . . I mean, people always argue about whether God's a man or a woman. I've heard that argument so many times, and I always say that God doesn't have a body and isn't either one. And here that's what they say, too, and it's the only other place where I've ever heard it. It makes me see things in a totally different light. And when Jesus washed the disciples' feet at the Last Supper—that was women's work back then. Women and slaves always did that, and—I don't know, I just think that Jesus was saying a lot of things that we're saying now, but the church just distorted them. The men in the church just distorted them for themselves at the time. It may be even the writers of the Bible distorted them—this is my own idea. I know it was divinely inspired, or whatever, but there's still human error, and there's still, you know, personal advancement. . . . And I was never allowed to say that. *Oh my gosh! That's heresy!* Because, I mean, I learned that from my mom. She's the one who told me that, and she said, "But don't say that at school" and all. And I was like, "I know better than to say that at school."

Kendra's self-censorship allowed her to remain at her school without being ostracized. The cost of this censorship, however, was a certain kind of loneliness. Kendra had believed that she was the only person thinking such thoughts about the Bible, the church, and women, and that she must therefore be strange or unusual. Fortunately, Kendra's mother helped her negotiate these differences of meaning strategically in different contexts. "I don't mean to upset anybody," Kendra said in reference to her changing notions of God and faith, "but I've got to think these things through for myself."

A True Faith, Not Just Religion

In their large-scale empirical study of adolescent religiosity, Christian Smith and Melinda Lundquist Denton report that, contrary to expectations, very few of the youth responding to a survey question considered themselves "spiritual but not religious." Smith and Denton expected to hear this phrase far more frequently among young people, who, they hypothesized, would belong to an age group disaffiliated from "organized religion." The young people in Smith and Denton's research sample expressed a kind of faith that the authors call "moral therapeutic deism," or religion as an affirmation of socially affirmed character traits and values, used as a means of handling personal difficulties and feeling good, all in relation to a nonspecific deity. Nevertheless, the young people in Smith and Denton's research sample for whom religious practices and ideas mattered did not identify themselves as "spiritual but not religious."[4]

In contrast, over half of the girls in this set of interviews defined religion by distinguishing it from faith and/or spirituality. Many girls distinguished between religion and spirituality in terms of a polarity between "organized religion" in its particularity (as a system of beliefs and doctrines, or as a particular church tradition) versus spirituality (a personally meaningful, internal experience, often of a more diffuse, open, and abstract nature).

In my questions to these girls, I did not make distinctions among the terms "faith," "religion," "belief," and "spirituality," and I tended to use the words somewhat interchangeably in order to listen for how the girls themselves might make distinctions of meaning among these terms.[5] This procedure did not stop the girls themselves from quickly distinguishing their own understandings of religion from what one girl termed "simple moralisms—you know, religion as a system of what-thou-shalt-not-do." Similarly, they rejected religion in the sense of mere outward form, "the kind where people dress up in fancy clothes and smile at each other once a week at church but don't have any inner experience of God or any outer expression of their faith."

What I found is that it was precisely because religion was so important to them that they refused the term "religious." Unlike Smith and Denton, who appear to equate teenagers' use of the phrase "spiritual but not religious" with an ungrounded or less serious "seeker" mind-set, I often heard young women use this phrase from a position *within* their Christian congregations and denominations, as a way to distinguish between a vibrantly experienced religious faith and the narrow meanings of the word "religious" that are common in the wider culture.[6]

Nearly all the girls interviewed spoke about faith primarily as an experience. For example, one of the more common ways to characterize "true" religion or faith was to describe it as an experience involving a person's heart. Using such language, Althea described a turning point where she had moved from a state of knowing *about* God to having an experience *of* God:

I had been to camp when I first became a Christian, so it's kind of like the place to go when I had my heart changed, or something.

People mean different things when they say, "When I first became a Christian." What do you mean when you say that?

I mean a personal experience with God, actually praying, and saying, "Lord, come into my heart," and [giving] my life to Him that way. . . . I felt stronger, like I felt stronger just from believing that He had done that.

Althea used a heart metaphor to describe the place of change and the place where God resides within herself. The link between religious use of this metaphor and its wider use to characterize the seat of feelings and passions suggests that, for girls like Althea, the affective dimension of faith is central to the experience of God.

Elaine made this connection clear as she described her conversion experience:

> It was the seventh grade, and I could tell you the exact day. It was totally amazing because I had prayed that prayer, "Jesus, clean my heart," before. Maybe it was the November before that, but it didn't mean anything, because there was something inside of me that was holding me back still, and until I got through that, I couldn't really ask Jesus to come in. He probably was there the whole time, but I couldn't feel Him.
>
> *What was keeping you from being able to do that?*
>
> I don't even remember. It might have even been how I felt towards my brother, because I hated him. I hated him with a passion. I would never say anything nice about him. I mean, I couldn't stand him. That was keeping me from a connection with God, because I couldn't go to Him unless I was totally free of all my sin, or whatever. I mean, not free of sin, but, you know, open to everything. Willing to forgive. After I had said whatever I needed to say, and I just said, "Forgive me for it," my life totally changed.

For Elaine, the heart was a place within the self where Jesus could reside after cleansing away what were to her unacceptable passions, such as hatred. The result of this cleansing for Elaine was that she became open, and her life "totally changed." Other girls spoke similarly of having their lives changed.

Many girls were reluctant to apply the word "religious" to their lived experience of consciousness of God and their day-to-day practices of faith. Marcia heard the word pejoratively. Asked if she considered herself to be a religious person, she replied:

> That's a hard question. I don't know. It depends on what you mean by "religious." I mean, I believe in God. I guess I believe there is somebody higher up there, you know? See, I believe in God, I believe in somebody out there. Something—He's out there, or She, you know, looking out for me. And I like knowing that somebody has a plan for me, but I don't know if I see myself as religious. That word carries a weight to me, "religious."

Kendra, in an animated tone of voice, also rejected application of the word "religious" to herself, even though she quickly professed her love of the United Methodist Church:

> I love it. I've grown up in it. But I don't consider myself a religious person. I really don't. I know the Bible front and back—I mean, I know everything about the Bible physically, but I don't consider myself a religious person. "Religious"—I don't really like that word, because to me "religious" means kind of barricaded in the church and to the church with other Christians, other people of your same race, background, religion, denomination. And going to church every day, and sitting in that little church with other white people, other upper-middle-class white people. Listening to the preacher tell you about forgiveness and grace and the love of God, and then maybe working on the Habitat [for Humanity] house once a year, on some weekend. And always bringing your cans [donations of nonperishable foods for the community food pantry]. But to me, that's not what we're called to do. That's a religious person to me, but that's not what God—that's not what Jesus wanted us to do. That's not what He said for us to do. So I don't really consider myself a religious person.

Kendra's move to redefine herself as not really a religious person was actually part of her larger redefinition of religion itself, whether this had to do with the tacitly defined activities of church people or with deeper notions based on "what Jesus wanted." In effect, her words were less a rejection of "religious" as a self-description than of inadequate, culturally normative understandings of what it means to be religious.

Other girls dealt in a similar way with denominational labels. For example, Brenda had recently decided that there was little integrity in applying a denominational label to herself when she knew so little about the denomination; the label, she asserted, was less important than the way of life:

> People ask me what I am. I just say I'm independent, because I don't know any of the Baptist customs, and I—and really I'm not sure if I even want to be in a religion [denomination]. I just want to believe in God. And I don't see why being a certain religion has anything to do with being a Christian. Because I understand there are all kinds of ways to serve God, instead of saying you're Baptist, and you really don't know anything about being Baptist. So—and really, I'm still looking for what I want to be. So I'm going to say "independent" until I find that out.

Again and again, girls made distinctions between religion connected to church life, which they sometimes described as "empty ritual" or "going through the motions," and faith or spirituality as *experienced* religion, involving a change of heart and a way of life. Julie described in some detail what this life change meant for her:

> Actually, I was saved after my seventh-grade year, so eighth grade is when I started my relationship with God. So my tenth-grade year, I learned more about God's love. So that's kind of the year of love to me, when I realized how much God loves me. And maybe that changed my perception of the world, and my perception of why I was here, maybe. To me, I was here to just be loved by God. And that's—it's really changed my, um, just the way I view life. Because it used to be, before, that it was kind of a thing you had to do. It was more of a *religion* before that, and it was more of just, I think, maybe something that I *had* to do. And that—it was kind of, I felt, like—you know, what God had called me to do, maybe. And after [realizing how much God loved], it was more of like—it was a relationship where I wanted to do it. And I wanted to know God and to love Him.

The word "religion," with its static connotations (for Julie) of being just something that had to be done, seemed unable to signify for her the affective dimensions and passions that she asserted as most important. As she put it, her conversion involved the turn from having a *religion* to having a *relationship*.

When Pam talked about her faith, she began by naming actions: "I see myself identifying needs and trying to do a lot of service." For Pam, the church was one place where she found meaningful opportunities for service. And yet she did not always feel comfortable identifying with the church:

> I consider myself a part of the *work* of the church but not of the *church*. The kind of hypocrisy, and things that go on, I know, in every church—the minister of that church, and a lot of the people, are very stuck in their ways. I see attitudes stuck. The ones that just make me so mad are prejudice and sexism, and those kinds of things really make me kind of mad. I don't want to identify with that, but then again I do want to—not with that, but with the good work of the church. I think that's good, because if you don't have people looking at the church and criticizing it, then you stay static.

Developmental psychologists have long noted the adolescent propensity, audible in Pam's words, for idealistic thinking and crusading against hypocrisy. Such critical speech is born of adolescents' heightened cognitive capacities for imagining the ideal or the hypothetical beyond what is concrete and actual in life. Here, Pam imagined and identified with the church as it should have been, critiquing the church as it was. It would be a mistake, however, to reduce Pam's passion for a more authentic Christian church to developmental features alone. Pam, like other girls in my research, hungered for faith in its communal forms to demonstrate coherence and integrity with its expressed beliefs.

Chelsea, the daughter of a Lutheran minister, offered another example of this critical perspective on the church:

> I consider myself a spiritual person. But "religious" has, like, connections, like, to the church and the devotions and, like—that you go along with what the church says, and what they say is right. But I don't really like that, even though I've been to church all my life. I mean, it's just sort of more like a community.
>
> *Religion is to you like that?*
>
> I mean, that's what I get out of it, but I don't like . . . all of the division between all of the different kinds of denominations.
>
> *What bothers you about that?*
>
> Just that people are so focusing on little differences, just little things, that aren't really even the focus or the core of Christianity, or whatever. And they just focus on that, and make that a big part, when it's just a small thing.
>
> *How, then, in your understanding, is being spiritual different from being religious?*
>
> Spiritual—I think about things, not just concrete, but things that are more abstract and hard to pin down.
>
> *Like what?*
>
> I don't know. Just going off and thinking. I don't even know what about—just thinking, instead of like religion, where you're bad to think.

Chelsea named a common concern of many girls about applying the term "religious" to themselves: it held conformist connotations that they rejected. The term's associations with churches suggested for some girls a lack of individual freedom to question and think, or an external conformity to particular practices of the group as a condition for inclusion.

For some girls, however, the word "spirituality" functioned as a synonym for "faith," and both, for them, were distinct from the term "religion." Courtney, for example, drew contrasts between the religion of church services in her Episcopal tradition, on the one hand, and faith, on the other hand, all the while maintaining the value of these religious services for what she called her own spirituality:

> To me, the church and the services were not necessarily the same thing as faith. Um, I sort of separate religion and faith a little bit—because, in confirmation especially, they taught us about the different services, and, um, you know, marriage and baptism and confirmation, and the Eucharist service, and all that kind of stuff. But the services were really more of a ritual for me than anything that really had meaning [for] spirituality. I mean, *now* that's completely different. I think the services help me to sort of identify my own spirituality. I think a lot of people are religious without having a whole lot of faith. [*Laughter.*] It's sort of a funny analogy that my sister and I came up with once. We call them "gas-station Christians." They go to church on Sundays to fill up for the week. To me, the ritual is nice because I've sort of memorized the service and, you know, then I can say it and listen to what I'm saying and take the meaning in it instead of just trying to keep up with the service. But I think a lot of people just go and say the words and never really think about what they're saying or why they're saying it. And so I think religion is sort of the ritualistic side of it, and faith is taking what you hear and internalizing and getting your own meaning out of it.

This group of young women who spoke of spirituality sought to differentiate their practices from empty ritual and institutional conformity, in favor of individually internalized meanings and relational and/or inner centers of authority. Developmental theorists talk helpfully about this phenomenon in terms of the fact that adolescents' renegotiation of their relationships with the people around them (parents, authorities, friends) also necessitates work toward reconfiguring their relationships with institutions like the church as they move away from uncritical embeddedness within the institution's norms and culture and toward a new self-responsibility and self-authorization.[7] Many among this group of girls were actively sorting out the relationship between their own faith and the received faith of their religious communities and traditions, making a distinction between religion and spirituality.

Time and time again in these interviews, girls struggled to come to terms with the gaps between religious ideas and religious practices, whether in their families, their congregations, or their own lives. As we have seen, for many girls this process involved disidentification with church-based or "organized" religion, as they often referred to it. Some of these girls tended to describe their religious practices as completely self-authored. That is, these girls viewed themselves more as fashioning their own unique brands of faith practices than as being formed in faith by anything "outside" them, whether that outside entity might be the family's religious teachings, the "collective effervescence"[8] of sociological understandings of religion, or some theological notion of revelation, such as those involving the work of God's Spirit.[9]

In other instances, though, girls remained identified and connected with their church traditions, claiming these as their own. But even when girls alluded to their faith practices' having been shaped by their denominational traditions, many of them, like Pam, still offered nuanced comments to qualify their definitions of religion. For these girls, faith remained connected *with*, but not uncritically embedded *within*, the received traditions of their churches. There may be a bit of normal adolescent hubris in the degree of self-authored faith claimed by some of these girls. Even so, it is necessary to respect the positive intent behind their efforts to construct and lay claim to a form of faith filled with meaning and integrity.

Left Behind by the Religious Right

As a further factor in the disdain for the term "religious" among so many girls in my interview group, these girls, growing up in the 1980s and 1990s, had also witnessed the ascendance of the Religious Right, and of the appeal of evangelical and fundamentalist groups, in the United States. The girls speaking in this set of interviews grew up in a society in which popular notions about what constitutes religion were heavily informed by a "conservative religious presence in the media,"[10] in the form of the so-called Electronic Church and other media used by the Religious Right. Not surprisingly, the term "religious" bore associations with these more conservative religious groups and their requirements of adherence to particular, narrow forms of piety in order for one to be included as a Christian. These girls wanted to be able to think and act according to their own faiths, without the encumbrance of the assumptions that come with the word "religion" in United States society today.

Marcia captured the gist of associations between the word "religious" and televangelism or conservative religion as she described her initial fears about attending YTI:

> The booklet [about YTI] implies that the kids are going to be like Bible bangers. Nobody here is. Everybody is just like me, you know?

What does that mean, everybody's just like you?

Same views. I mean, they're not, like, "Well, the Bible says this and this and this and this." I thought everybody would be real religious—you know, "You can't do that, you can't say that, you can't think that," because—you know—just, like, really really super-religious.

What is a really religious person?

I don't know. Somebody who just—like, every word that comes out of their mouth is, like, Bible-related. Everything you say, they try to refute it with somewhere in the Bible. They try to, like, force their opinions on you.

None of the girls spoke directly about the influence of conservative religion's ascendancy on her own definition of religion. Nevertheless, that ascendancy forms a significant part of the cultural backdrop, and of popular culture's discourse about religion. Girls like Marcia and Chelsea wanted to define religion in ways that invited probing and questioning, ways that privileged experience, and ways that upheld their freedom to hold views that dissented from those of the majority in their churches, without the threat of exclusion. The inability of many girls to continue using the words "religious" and "religion" to reference their own faith is something that points to the dominance of popular culture's meanings of these terms; indeed, popular culture would fix these definitions around a particular set of moralistic meanings that are less descriptive of Christian faith in its greater diversity than of the contemporary political co-opting of religion by the conservative Protestant subculture associated with the Religious Right.

Walking the Walk

Against such fixity, girls in my study offered more fluid descriptions of their faith that defined religion as an "owned," personal experience involving commitments to action. Kathy, for example, was asked, "How would you describe your present faith?" "Questioning," she responded.

Moving. Kind of a journey. Going from. Seems like it is never-ending. Every time you have a question, and every time you find the answer to a question, you get a new question. My faith—it's personal, it's mine.

Kathy's claim that her faith was "personal" functioned in part to protect her from efforts by others to define it for her, or to tell her what it should mean.

Ellen, who lived in a small southeastern town, accepted her community's particular definition of what it meant to act like a Christian ("not drink, and not do all that"), but she also levied a further claim about faith:

> There's people who say they are Christian, but how can some people say they are Christian when they don't really walk the walk? I mean, people can *act* like they are [Christians]—not drink, and not do all that—but, to me, you also have to be spiritual, and really feel it, to be religious.

Or take Andrea, who in junior high school had been "very religious":

> I knew the Bible frontward and backwards. I knew everything *about* God, but I didn't know *God*.

In short, girls like Kathy, Ellen, and Andrea manifested a strong concern with authentic religious experience as a primary marker of faith. As a group, the girls in these interviews displayed considerable investment in defining the nature and meaning of their religiosity in ways that they understood to be self-chosen. Girls sought alternative language, such as "spiritual," to describe themselves, and they often defined their faith in terms of its difference from the participation of their parents or other adults in "organized religion." This work of naming their faith and describing its significance in their lives was a practice that some girls in the group used to resist overly narrow definitions of faith that functioned to exclude people. Instead, these fifty girls offered more open and fluid ways of naming their faith.

What all this talk of "religious" versus "spiritual" points to is that these girls were deeply immersed in struggles to bring about coherence between their emerging beliefs and their actions in the world. For these girls, a central religious issue was how to live with integrity, in such a way that they actually did what they believed in. Many of these sixteen-, seventeen-, and eighteen-year-old girls were struggling to find authentic ways to practice their faiths, and they were poignantly critical of hypocrisy in their homes and churches. Faith, to them, meant lining up their beliefs with their actions so that there was no contradiction between how they thought about God and how they lived in the world, even while many of them recognized the impossibility of fulfilling this demand at all times and in all places. Still, more congruence between the "inner person" and the outer life mattered to them. They were hypercritical of empty religious gestures divorced from lived, felt experience. They were not content with a religion of going through the motions; rather, they wanted recognizable connections between their beliefs and their ways of life.

What Shall We Do with Our Lives?

The question "What's next?" loomed large in the minds of the seventeen-year-old girls participating in YTI's summer academy. Going into their senior year of high school, these girls were already filling out college applications or making other decisions about what they would be doing at the end of their high school careers. Their faith was strongly implicated in most of these girls' decisions about where to go to school, or what kind of work to prepare for; they saw their lives as "having a purpose that is part of the purpose of God."[11] In short, they expressed a sense of *vocation*, of being called by God to use their lives in meaningful ways that would make a difference in the world.

These girls sometimes talked in general or vague terms about a sense of "call," or direction for their lives, coming from God. For the most part, however, they expressed the belief that their lives were meaningful and purposive by talking about the kinds of work in adulthood they wanted to prepare for. Julie, for example, noted the relationship between the kinds of gifts she sees in herself and the various kinds of work she might do:

> I think God put me on this earth for a purpose, to do something. You know, I may be here debating what I'm going to major in at college, but what I eventually decide, I think, is what God wants me to do. And God sent me here for a certain purpose, whether—like, now, I'm thinking, between political science and sociology, or social work or something like that. I really feel that I—I feel like I have leadership skills, and I'd like to work with people. I'm good at communicating, and I think I have a unique understanding of people that others may not. And I think that God really did that for me for a purpose. There was a reason that I had the family I did, that I've gone through every-thing that I've gone through, and it's all coming to form, like, my eventual goal, my eventual job that I'm going to go into—that's going to affect people. So I think I've touched people, I think I've helped people, and I think that everything I did has meaning, so my life has definite meaning.

A common theme in many girls' ideas was the thought that the ultimate human vocation is to love God; several girls echoed Susan's notion:

> God isn't here for us; *we're* here for *God*. Loving God is the main purpose for humans.

The question debated across these interviews was how people could best manifest their love of God in their lives. Kendra argued with the idea of love for God as the primary human calling. She saw it as an abdication of the human responsibility to love other people in need:

> I heard this song about the only reason humans are alive is to learn to love God. And I don't think that's true. Well, I guess that's *sort of* true, but I also think that we're here to make sure everyone has chances, you know. Because God—sure, God is in control, but we *have responsibility* for each other, and I really think that we do. I think that we're here to try to make sure that everybody gets a fair shot at God and life and, well—and basic living conditions. That's *my* purpose in life, to try my best to make sure—I mean, the poor are always going to be with us, like it says in the Bible. It also says that we're called to help the poor and the hungry. So I think—I guess that's why I'm here.

Such ideas—that they had a call from God to make a difference, to serve others, to care for the vulnerable—were a key ingredient of these girls' faith practices and beliefs. The girls enacted their convictions through service in churches' soup kitchens and in homeless shelters. They organized chapters of Amnesty International in their high schools. They marched with such groups such as People for the Ethical Treatment of Animals (PETA). They spent time as high school mentors to children in Head Start programs, and they read stories to children at the libraries in their communities.

Jennifer expressed her strong sense that God was calling her to use her life in some direction; it was just not clear to her yet what that direction might be:

> I used to want to be a lawyer, and then my feelings changed, because I like to listen to people. I want to open up a clinic—you know, like, in a city or somewhere, where they could just get counseling, you know. And I'd like to be a minister of music, that plays music for a church, and teaches music. I hope God has something to make up my mind about! I think He's got a plan for me.

In *Lives to Offer*, my coauthor Dori Grinenko Baker and I explore more fully the issue of vocation in relation to youth ministry. For that work, we drew on interviews with girls as well as boys at the Youth Theological Initiative, to make the claim that ministry with youth ought to focus on helping adolescents discover how they can offer their lives meaningfully in a needy, problem-filled world. But the emphasis on finding one's calling or vocation came through in a distinctive way in the interviews with girls, and the girls who were my research partners were not just thinking about the kinds of careers or work they wanted. Many of them expressed the idea that we are put on this earth to make a difference, and they described their religious practices in terms of their efforts to live out the call from God to use their lives in certain ways. They differed in their understanding of how God's purposes unfold in individual lives, but most of these girls affirmed the idea that God has a plan for every person.

Already, approaching their final year of high school, as they articulated how to offer their lives, many of the girls also thought about how to combine meaningful work with having children and a family.

"I want to be a doctor, but I'm not sure how that will go along with being a mom," Mary Anne said. "I'm leaving it open, what I will do with my life. I know I could do anything. But I want to choose work that fits with raising a family."

Similarly, Alyssa imagined "figuring out some kind of work that will let me relocate if I need to—like, if I am married, and we need to move. I want to be able to be flexible in my life, including my work. Serve God, and be flexible—how's that for a combination?"

An important part of the religious lives of adolescent girls concerns this sense of being called to make a difference, to offer their lives in some meaningful way. It is noticeable that when these young women imagined what kinds of work they might do as adults, they did not place work in a vacuum. Instead, they imagined work along with family relationships as a key factor. Thus, when these girls thought about their callings, their musings included fitting in a family as part of the response to the call.

Imagining God's Desire

Religious imagination is, at least in part, the capacity to use linguistic and other forms of imagery to express the ineffable. Walter Brueggemann writes that human knowing is the work of imagination, defined as "the human capacity to picture, portray, receive, and practice the world in ways other than it appears to be at first glance when seen through a dominant, habitual, unexamined lens."[12] Where *imagination* is concerned, religious imagination is a way of knowing that involves conjuring up the impossible and the unknown, putting people's desires and hopes into imagistic form (language, dreams, art, music, and the like) and action. And where the *religious* aspect is concerned, religious imagination brings this activity to bear on transcendence and mystery as well as on the actual material conditions through which people experience life, and it engages the primary symbols and metaphors of religious communities. Thus religious imagination involves dimensions that are conscious and unconscious, tangible and symbolic.

The religious imagination of these girls often involved symbols and metaphors from Christian tradition, imaginatively reworked in fresh ways. What was most interesting, their practices of religious imagination often intersected with their social concerns. This intersection was evident in Kendra's speech as she discussed the place of sacraments in her worship practices. Earlier in her interview, she had talked about her emerging awareness of the suffering of homeless people and her desire to be an agent for change. Now, turning to talk about sacraments, she framed the central meaning of communion in terms of its abolition of class distinctions:

> Communion is very important to me. It's always been very important to me. Communion—communion of saints. Because, to me, that's the whole idea, the communion with each other. That's the whole idea, that you're not alone. We're all only *in* the body of Christ. We *are* the body of Christ. We're all saints, and that's real important. It's kind of an equalizing thing for me. Like the Apostles' Creed, we always say, "The communion of saints, the forgiveness [of sins]." And I never understood "the saints" the way our church interprets it. It means everyone is a saint. So whether you make a hundred thousand dollars a year or fifty thousand or below twenty thousand dollars a year, it doesn't matter. You're still the same in communion, at the altar. Taking the bread—everybody needs that. You can't pay for it. You can't get a better—you can't get a better part of the body of Christ, a better part of the blood. It's all the same. It's very important to me, and I always feel like when I go up to the rail, it's my favorite time. It's the first Sunday of every month, and it's so important to me. I feel like that's the time to start over. I can start over again. I feel renewed. It's real important to me.

Kendra, working with images from liturgical and creedal sources, saw beyond the face value of the symbols associated with the sacrament of communion and imagined the church as a place where status differences became relativized. For her, communion functioned as a marker of inclusion of people from different socioeconomic groups. It was the great equalizer because, as Kendra said, one cannot pay at the communion rail for a better part of the body or blood of Christ.

At another point in her interview, Kendra told about times of financial struggle in her family and of feeling "second class" at her church because only one of her parents was involved (given her church's unspoken norms, one parent's choice not to participate left her feeling as if she came from an inferior family). Therefore, the role of communion as a marker of inclusion was especially important to her. In Kendra's utopic imaging of this sacrament, she pictured a community in which all are fed according to their need, not according to their ability to purchase bread. In effect, her sacramental practice shifted the pattern of meaning embodied in the sacrament of communion, from a one-dimensional focus on the bread itself as the body of Christ to a renewed, expanded vision of both the bread and the people who participate as the body of Christ, reaching across markers of exclusion.

Similarly, Michelle related her beliefs about communion as a marker of inclusion as she told about her experience of defying efforts to exclude her because of religious difference. She attended a Catholic high school in which all students took part in a weekly mass. Michelle was not Roman Catholic but Presbyterian. Asked what that was like for her, she replied, "It's very difficult trying not to get angry. And I feel hurt a lot." (The sacrament is not supposed to be given to non-Catholics.)

> I do go forward to participate anyway. I mean, people say I shouldn't, because it's a respect thing, but it's not to me, it's not respect.
>
> *What is it to you?*
>
> Well I believe in *God*, and everybody else is supposed to, but [communion is] the symbol of God to me, and it's not a symbol of Catholicism or Presbyterianism, or—it's for all people of God, and as long as you believe that, then I don't see why not. But I feel looked at all the time whenever I walk up there. I mean, I know that the priest—no, *everyone*—knows that I'm not Catholic. And they serve me. They serve me. But I've got friends, they say, "Why do you do that?" And I'll explain it over and over and over and over again, and they still don't understand it.

In one sense, being in this situation—a Protestant believer in a Roman Catholic worship setting—provided Michelle with an opportunity she may well have welcomed: the chance to register an act of protest by physically walking forward to receive communion every week, over the objections of canon law and her questioning friends. At the same time, she obviously did not do so unthinkingly, or without some cost to herself. This practice of faith was important enough to Michelle that she asserted, through her actions, that the meanings she held for this sacrament were valid. She did so even in the face of opposition and criticism from peers. And although she did not have the support of her Catholic friends, at least she experienced the tacit support of the priest who served her each week.

In effect, Michelle's resistance of one set of meanings—those embodied in the practice of excluding non-Catholics from participation in the Eucharist—accomplished a practical transformation in this rite at the local level. That is, she obviously did not change this practice for the whole Catholic Church, but her actions did transform the sacramental practice in her school's chapel for one brief moment each week. She grounded her practice in her utopian imagining of the sacrament as being "for all people of God," a perspective clearly beyond the realities of the present Eucharistic practice of many churches. Such visions *are* utopian in the sense that they conjure up an imaginary situation far more wonderful and hopeful than what we know in our actual experience.

Some theologians critique utopian thinking as playing into a pie-in-the sky religion that encourages people to be satisfied with poor conditions in this life, on the promise of a reward awaiting them in heaven. That is one way to see utopia. But, having listened to what these girls said as they reimagined the meanings and transformed the practices of well-worn rites and symbols of the faith, I use the term "utopia" in a positive way, in connection with the hopeful visions of new and better forms of community of which these girls dreamed. This is one way to imagine God's desire.

Mikela brought her practice of religious imagination to bear on issues of social class, first describing her experience of having been brought up by her mother and her grandmother in a poverty-stricken urban area:

> You know, I don't remember us being poor, like we see some of the people now. I basically got what I wanted, like toys, 'cause I was in this program in this day care center.

As her interview continued, she described various experiences of struggle, including painful family relationships, economic hardship, and experiences with violence and sexual harassment. Sorting through various ways of understanding God's relationship to human suffering, she spoke about God as a loving, caring friend who stays involved with suffering people and yet "sees the big picture beyond what we see":

> I used to believe that if you were saved, you wouldn't have that much suffering in your life. But then I started reading different Bible stories, and I learned that suffering is just a part of life, and you can't avoid suffering. You know, I know—like, some people—I've heard people here say it, and I've heard people everywhere say it, that if there was a God, there wouldn't be poverty, there wouldn't be this or that. But I believe there is a God, but those things are just in the world. I know it's easy to say that if there was a God, people wouldn't be starving, but I think that God just knows. I mean, our minds are so small that we can't comprehend everything He has in store for us. So I'm not going to set back and say it's His fault, because I don't [believe that].

In short, Mikela imagined a "beyond" to God's providential care that lies outside human purview. She made sense of the suffering in her own life and in others' lives by adopting the notion that "those things are just in the world," and she pictured a God who knows more than humans know and who has something else "in store for us." This stance, far from a pie-in-the-sky religion that pacifies dissatisfaction with injustice, appeared to operate for Mikela as a kind of critical principle in relation to the suffering of human experience. Mikela did not see herself as a victim, despite the significant hardships she had known, nor did she see God as blameworthy. Instead, she imagined a God who is more than the present givenness of life alone.

Another example of how these girls used practices of imagination in the service of new and hopeful ways to make sense of the world came from Pam. In her interview, she spoke at length about the difficulties of her teen years, including the traumatic death of her friend's mother, her own depression, and stressful relationships with boyfriends. Pam spoke of how attending a Quaker meeting had caused her to recognize the importance of the cross for her Methodist tradition, and for her own life of faith, and she remade its meaning in light of her own struggles:

> *Are there any particular religious ideas, symbols, or rituals that are important to you?*
>
> I think symbolism is really important, personally. I think that might have really a lot to do with me being Methodist. We went to the Quaker meeting yesterday, and they didn't have a cross anywhere in

the church. That's one thing that really struck me. You didn't have that constant reminder somewhere that—that just really struck me, that the cross is really important to me.

What does the cross mean to you?

It's a great symbol of hope. Of resurrection. It's something that's been real present, so I never thought about it not being there. To me, seeing other people's deaths, especially the kind of death I've seen, it makes me feel like there has to be something else beyond that. I don't believe that the spirit and the soul just die. Even if people don't believe in heaven, although I personally do, just their influence stays around on someone in some kind of way. . . . I had never seen a Christian church without a cross. And someone asked about it. The leader at the Quaker meeting, he just said they didn't feel the symbolism was real important, and that completely struck me in that—like, I think it's one of the most important messages about the Christian faith, and hope. For me, it's that thing about not being afraid of death, since Christ told the disciples that he would come again and raise us all. If you don't have that kind of hope—that something is going to be there after you die—it's going to take you a long time to accept your death.

Practices of religious imagination take available symbols and metaphors—such as the cross, in this case—and infuse them with significance beyond their face value. Pam did this as she worked from the symbol of the cross as the instrument of Jesus' death to its implications of hope and resurrection for others, which, she went on to suggest, helped her to cope with the horror of death as she knew it. Pam's example is one among many of the ways these girls spoke of employing their faith practices in relation to the problems and struggles of their lives.

Prayer as Hope, Praying for Change

For some girls, prayer was a meaningful way to be connected with God. Others were not so sure that prayer really accomplished anything. Jan voiced the latter sentiment when she said of prayer, "I do it, but while I do it, I wonder if I'm just talking to myself."

Still another group of girls looked at prayer as a way to make a difference in the world and in the lives of people. Courtney thought aloud about how prayer worked toward change in her life and in the world:

Well, I don't know. Most of the time, I just talk. And I think that in some sort of way, He—uh, God—sort of affects what I think a little bit. You know, it's sort of a one-sided conversation because I don't actually hear Him answer. But, you know, sometimes what I say—it's not answered immediately. It might be a few days, a week, a month, before I get an answer to a question. But I believe that eventually I'll always be able to get an answer from God. And so it's a long conversation.

Not all the girls in the group prayed. But those girls in the study who talked about prayer as a valued practice all expressed strong convictions that prayer makes a difference or can create change. Such change, they posited, took place in relation to the human parties to prayer—the girls themselves, or others for whom they prayed.

Althea's practice of prayer was closely tied to her theology of God's providential plan for humanity. We had the following exchange while I was listening to her story about a close friend dying from a chronic health condition:

When you pray to God and you are concerned for somebody like your friend, what do you think God does with that concern?

[Long pause.] I guess God turns some of that concern over into trust that I am supposed to have—that He will take care of it, I guess.

Okay. I'm wondering if you think that when you pray to God, it changes what God will do.

[Another long pause.] I don't know about that. I sorta think that God already has a plan, and of course He knows what everything is going to be in the beginning, so I guess He knows how it is going to turn out. And so it was kind of like He was planning to do it anyway.

Does it matter, then, to pray?

Yeah, I think—this is deep! [Laughter.] I guess in some ways it's good to pray. It brings people together, at least, in a sense, and it's always good to feel that you have a purpose, you know, and that you are together for a cause. Maybe it does change the way God feels. I can't help but see that He already knows what is going to happen, though, so that's confusing.

Prayer may or may not "change the way God feels," Althea said, but it remained for her an important and purposive action. Here, Althea experienced a dilemma. On the one hand, she fully believed that God already had a plan, with foreknowledge of what would happen. On the other hand, she believed in the importance of prayer to transform reality, even the reality of God. In the midst of this dilemma, her practice of prayer and her reflection on her practice included the assertion that prayer, whatever its mechanism of efficacy, acts transformatively in people's lives. For Althea—who also, in her interview, described relationships with friends who suffered disabilities, told about her own painful experience of losing loved ones, and spoke about betrayals by friends—the assertion of prayer's power to transform, through the purposive bringing together of a community, reflected an imaginative practice reaching beyond what was known to be possible and toward an uncertain, hoped-for potential for change.

What comes through clearly in their responses to questions about religious imagination and prayer is that these girls portrayed their religious practices as practices of justice. For many of the girls, Christian faith was most centrally about working to make real on earth the new reign of God announced by Jesus. They saw themselves living their faith by recognizing various kinds of injustice in the world and making efforts to transform it, whether on the small scale of individual prayers for those who were sick, poor, and hungry or on the larger scale of social movements.

Family Ties

Girl talk on faith can sometimes sound as if a girl's efforts to shape her religious life take place, at best, in isolation from her family's efforts and, at worst, come about in opposition to her family's beliefs and practices. What can be difficult in a family is that an adolescent girl often uses her own household as the test kitchen for cooking up impassioned critiques of the church or organized religion. The family can become the prime location for her to gauge the hypocrisy when practices fail to live up to ideals. Her home may become ground zero for her running commentary on the inadequacies of the faith in which she was brought up.

It may help for her parents to remember that adolescence is only one season in the life of their daughter, and in their own parenting, and that it can be a very constructive season in spite of the conflicts it may also bring. For their daughter, adolescence is the season for owning and internalizing faith, for claiming it as her own—often by critiquing the inadequacies, perceived and real, of others' faith practices. Perhaps for her parents, the years of parenting an adolescent girl can be a season for renewing faith. After all, it will surely be a time of listening in on, and sometime being in dialogue with, their daughter, whose critical voice masks her own renegotiations in search of a faith that is relational, that has integrity, that gives her life a purposeful orientation, and that enacts justice.

Parents often report feeling that they have diminishing influence over or connection with the religious lives of their daughters, but the girls in these interviews constantly invoked their parents' names. Sometimes they pointed out how different their own beliefs were from those of their parents. At other times they spoke of their parents when discussing their images of God, using stories from their own family experiences of care and support, or sometimes of stress and struggle, to explain what they meant when they called God "Father" or, less frequently, "Mother." Many of these daughters mentioned talking with their parents about religious questions, and they worried about hurting their parents, or being rejected by them, because of differences in religious beliefs and practices. They also relied on their parents to help them sort out their beliefs. Clearly, the influence of parents in the religious lives of their adolescent daughters is different from what it was when their daughters were little girls. But parents certainly are not without a significant role in their daughters' adolescence, if we believe what these girls had to say. Talk about family members, especially parents, remains integral to girl talk on faith.

Reflections

As I review the variety of ways in which these girls who were my research partners talked about faith, I am reminded of what a powerful time the teen years can be in the shaping of a girl's life of faith. I especially recall the excitement of new levels of making meaning during those years. For example, Kendra's words about the radical welcome that God extends in the Christian sacrament of Holy Communion—"You can't pay for it . . . you can't get a better part of the body of Christ, a better part of the blood"—call to mind a similar "aha" moment of my adolescence, when, as a member of a church youth group, I participated in celebrating communion with a group of migrant farmworkers on Virginia's Eastern Shore. In parallel to Jesus' use of bread and wine in his time, we used cornbread and cola as the common table elements in our own context. Our group had been working to ready a building that would serve as a day care center for the migrant laborers' children while the children's parents worked for low wages to harvest crops under difficult conditions. In that simple and unconventional Eucharist, I suddenly grasped new levels of meaning concerning the sacrament: through our sharing, first of our labor, and then of the bread used in this communion celebration, people whose economic and cultural differences ordinarily kept them from encountering each other ended up coming together in the welcome of Christ's table. There, those differences ceased to have dividing power.

I recall the amazement with which it suddenly occurred to me that in this sacrament, ordinary things—cornbread and cola—became holy and were there for all to share in the odd little new community that we and our hosts, the farmworkers, constituted around the communion table. That moment sealed forever in my awareness new meanings of the sacrament, connected not merely to my individual ideas or beliefs about God but also to communal practices of justice that matter to vulnerable people in the world.

Like the adolescent girls whose reflections on faith appear in the pages of this chapter, my peers and I criticized the hypocrisy of religious organizations, and we questioned religious practices that seemed to us to lack authenticity. It mattered to have adults around us who could hear our critiques not simply as a threat to their cherished beliefs (well, at least not all the time) but also as an opportunity for faith's renewal and transformation. It mattered to have adults (in some cases parents, but often others) around us who were willing to raise questions that might have remained at tacit and unreflective levels of awareness if someone had not asked, "What *do* you think it means to talk about God as being a Trinity?" From my present-day position as an adult invested in relationships with young people, I am aware of the risks those adults took—the vulnerability of not knowing, of appearing foolish or inauthentic or, worse yet, boring in the face of a young person's faith quest. The voices of these girls give me courage and hope because they remind me that faith is about knowing and acting in the world, and it is also about relationships. These girls remind me that faith concerns a lifelong quest for coherence between what we believe and how we live our beliefs. Their voices push to the foreground the demand that the things we do fit with the things we say. They invite a renewed embracing of the sense of purposeful living—what the Christian tradition terms "vocation"—that connects with the purposes of God and is bigger than my own individual life. And they call me to a vibrant reimagining of God's desires for justice, a faith put to work toward transformation, so that all will truly be welcome at the table of life.

3

GIRL TALK ON GENDER

DENISE STRODE INTO THE ROOM wearing tight-fitting, low-cut jeans and a cropped T-shirt that pulled up when she sat down, showing off her midriff. On the front of the shirt the words LOOK BUT DON'T TOUCH appeared in fancy cursive script surrounded by tiny flowers. The back of the shirt contained a similar border of flowers, now surrounding bold block letters reading I'LL LET YOU KNOW IF I CHANGE MY MIND. With a quick apology for being late, she launched into recounting the lunch-table conversation from which she had just come:

> We were talking about whether there is still a double standard for girls and for guys—you know, like, different rules that apply to you, depending on your sex. That was definitely the case when my mom and dad were in high school. You should hear *their* stories. I don't know that it's still true today, at least not at the personal level, for me.

She spoke energetically on the topic, though, giving several examples of what she called society's double standards:

> Men can go on to professional sports, but most women's sports don't go beyond college teams. And I think it's still true in some places that women get paid less than men, although I don't get paid less where I work just because I'm female. It probably does happen, though. Then there's the whole thing about how women get paid less in their jobs that are, like, elementary school teaching or child care—well, maybe the *jobs* get valued less *because* they are done by women. I'm not sure which comes first. Some of the guys at lunch were saying, "What about the Bible, where it says women should be silent in church?" I think they were joking, but, you know, there is still a big double standard in some churches. My church is very strong on women.

We have a woman priest. Anyway, double standards—of course, there
are still differences for some people, in terms of what girls and guys
can do, you know, physically.

Denise described the sexual double standard at her high school, whereby
some girls were "labeled as sluts for the same things that guys win medals
for doing. But," she continued, "most people have moved past that kind
of thing."

I asked her to tell me about the writing on her tee shirt.

Oh, that. [*Laughter.*] It's nothing. It's a joke, a way girls make it
sound like they call the shots. I mean, I do call the shots about my
own body, so that part's not a joke. It's that on one side I'm saying,
like, no way you are getting near me—but don't you wish you could?
Flirting. Then, on the other side, I'm saying, I'm the one making the
decisions here, so don't mess with me—but keep trying, 'cause I could
always change my mind. That's what it's like to be a girl now. As my
mom would say, not as many double standards, but lots of double
messages.

Denise's comments reflect the current context in which adolescent girls
attempt to make sense of gender—their own and others'—and embody its
meanings in their everyday lives. It is a context in which meanings, ideas,
and attitudes are in transition, and sometimes in conflict. And, just as
there are many different ways girls understand and live out what being
female means to them, so too are there multiple perspectives within the
Christian faith on gender and gender differences. For instance, girls participating in faith communities may find resources that support their well-
being as young women; they may also find religious authorizations of
gender inequality that undermine their thriving. There is no singular pattern to the intersections of gender and faith. But, among a number of differences the girls expressed in their interviews, all of them made it clear
that they had a great deal at stake in both of these intersecting elements.
For these girls, being female and being Christian were two key aspects of
identity, and both aspects were integral to the sense of self that defined
who they were in the world.

What It Means to Be Female

Although they cared intensely about the subject of gender and could be
quite passionate in expressing their ideas about it, the girls who talked
with me had a tough time at the outset naming what it meant to them to

be girls. A surprising number expressed initial astonishment at the question, making statements like "That's not something I've tried to put into words before" or "I don't know what to say—I wouldn't know how to begin." Nicole gave voice to that kind of surprise when she responded forcefully, "What kind of a question is that? You can't say what it is, or what it means, to be female. You just are. You are a girl. Or you aren't."

One girl sought clarification of my question about the significance she attributed to being female:

> Do you mean, like, how do I become a woman? Like, when my mother gave me the sex talk, explained periods to me, and how girls can get pregnant, and then said something like "So now that you've got your period, you are a woman." Is that what this question is about?

She went on to describe sex education in her school as "the place where we talk about that stuff, but it's basically a plumbing lesson. . . . We only talk about how it works, never how it feels or what it means."

Little wonder, then, that girls have so much difficulty expressing their understanding of girlhood and womanhood, when they have been invited to talk about these aspects of identity primarily in anatomical terms. Joan Jacobs Brumberg, in *The Body Project,* her powerful social history of American girls, notes that "hygiene, not sexuality," has become the chief focus of discourse between mothers and daughters about the transition from girlhood to womanhood: "At the moment when they begin to menstruate, American girls and their mothers typically think first about the external body—what shows and what doesn't—rather than about the emotional and social meaning of the maturation process."[1] This reality was reflected in the initial responses of several girls to questions about gender, as they revealed themselves to be experts in the science of reproductive anatomy and biology but novices when it came to articulating the meanings and significance that being a girl held for them.

Once the girls got past their initial surprise, however, most of them had quite a lot to say about the various meanings they attached to being female. Michelle began tentatively, as if she had never put her thoughts into words before:

> Female—you're born that. Woman, you have to grow into, I think. It happens through life experiences, I think . . . surviving, just getting through—like, being strong, you know. Just being able to handle yourself. Taking responsibility, and so forth.

For Michelle, a person acquired the identity of woman through experiences that required strength, competence in the face of difficulty, and a sense of character.

"You're born a female, but you show that you're a woman by acting like one," Michelle reiterated.

As she spoke, her voice gradually took on the more confident tone of one who had knowledge to offer, even if, up until that moment, it had been unarticulated knowledge. What Michelle intuitively knew and expressed by distinguishing between the terms "female" and "woman" parallels a key assertion of contemporary scholars who study gender: biological differences do sort people into the sex categories of male and female, but the term "gender" refers to the meanings that a particular culture or society gives to those differences. Thus when we call someone a girl or a boy, a woman or a man, much more is referenced than anatomical distinctions. These terms conjure up a whole host of associations that include everything from competencies to colors, emotions to intelligence, and over time such associations come to be connected with these sex categories. At the same time that these meanings reflect what is already true of at least some people who fit the sex category of male or female (nurturing women, for example, or physically active boys), they also play a role in shaping our perspectives on what constitutes maleness or femaleness. Accordingly, the meanings that come to be associated with one sex category or the other play an important role in establishing the power relationships between these two groups. What Michelle knew is that sex differences certainly refer to biology, but gender differences are socially and culturally constructed, the product of a society's norms regarding what these differences *mean* and how they operate to shape relationships and experiences.

The related terms "masculine" and "feminine" describe social norms regarding what constitutes *appropriate* gender traits and behaviors. A particular behavior or trait—softness, for example—may be attributed to women so that the appearance of being soft is considered feminine in some cultures. When a person displays traits or behavior that are gender-incongruent, meaning that these traits or behavior do not fit the category (male or female) to which the person belongs, he or she may be accused of acting in an unfeminine or unmasculine way. Such accusations derive from behavior that disrupts the often implicit, socially agreed-upon categories of what is appropriate, and supposedly natural, for males or females. Almost all the girls with whom I spoke gave examples of occasions when they had trespassed the conventionally defined boundaries of femininity. Nevertheless, some of the same girls had obviously internalized and accepted conventional notions of masculine and feminine as givens of human sexual identity.

Jennifer, for example, an African American seventeen-year-old from a southern Baptist background, was quick to distinguish between the concepts of masculinity and femininity as a means of explaining what mattered to her about her own gender identity—namely, the idea that it was simply "natural." For Jennifer, notions of masculinity and femininity expressed underlying, innate differences between men and women. In her eyes, a woman who failed to follow the conventional expectations for femininity was not being "real" or was acting against her true nature:

> A feminine woman would be more reserved, maybe. Like, if it were something very serious that she wouldn't believe in, then she would speak out. But she wouldn't be ready to fight, or wouldn't be able to cause pain or want to hurt anybody, but just make sure her voice was heard. So I think that's more feminine. I'm not saying that men are noncaring. Okay, a woman who acts like, who wants to be something else—I'm not saying she wants to be a man—but she wants to be so rough, like, she wants to have a rough exterior. Maybe she's trying to block in her real feelings. To me, masculinity—I see it as being physically strong and, um, let me see—someone who is not shaken by situations.

As Jennifer began to qualify her statements in midsentence, her words sounded hesitant. Perhaps she was beginning to reflect critically on her previously unexamined assumptions about what was natural.

But what about girls who engaged in behavior or displayed traits that they themselves readily described as masculine? These girls, using a different logic, contended that even if a girl acted in a masculine way, she would still be female, but the behavior or quality would continue to be labeled masculine. Some girls, one explained, have "more of a mixture in what they do." Thus girls like Jessica found themselves in a quagmire when they attempted to explain what made certain characteristics masculine or feminine, apart from their conventional associations with males and females:

> *Are there any things that you do as part of being female that you particularly like?*
>
> Huh. Actually, I'm more of a tomboy, so that's kind of a hard question. You see, I just got back from lifting weights. [Laughter.] That's kind of masculine, I always thought.

Well, you know, that raises an interesting question about the way you are defining these terms.

I know. I never thought about it before. I just always kind of accepted it. I guess I am kind of traditional in that aspect. Although I don't— I see me breaking tradition. But I guess that's how I've always seen it.

Hmm. Okay. What does it mean to call weightlifting masculine, if you do it?

Hah! I don't know! This interview tape is going to be really contra-dicted. [Laughter.] I'm probably going to contradict myself so many times! Confusing issues for me, I guess. I guess I don't really see that much difference between men and women, I guess.

Jessica's last words illustrate what happened for many girls when they were invited to articulate their previously unexamined understandings of gender differences. They noticed contradictions in their own perspectives, expressed discomfort with these tensions, and then posited tentative new views in an effort to clear up the inconsistencies. In this way, they engaged in the active creation of new meanings as they frequently used these inter-views to articulate and try on new perspectives. At a minimum, this fact suggests the importance of creating opportunities for girls to articulate their tacit understandings of gender, both with peers and with concerned, contemplatively listening adults.

Several of the girls who spoke with me described, and occasionally showed, flowery tattoos or body piercings as examples of what they had done to their bodies to express being female. Although they all agreed that having a tattoo or a piercing did not make them female per se, the particular appearance of such body art was an expression of femininity:

See this little rose? It's right on my hip, right here. It's small. I had that done earlier this summer. My mom doesn't know about it, or she would probably kill me. Well, to me it means, like, a sign of being pretty, kind of an expression of how I feel I am as a woman, or whatever.

Asked what makes a particular tattoo symbol masculine or feminine, this girl replied, "If it's on a girl, it's feminine."

Some girls actively recognized the power of culture to shape their gen-der perspectives. They described society, rather than individual choices, as determining what gets labeled masculine or feminine. Roxanne, for example, who described herself as "a lesbian with a boyfriend," spoke about the differences between her personal experience and socially defined gender characteristics:

> *What makes something masculine or feminine, then?*
>
> What society says—if crying is feminine, it's because society said so. If being strong is masculine, it's because society said so. Basically, weakness is supposed to be feminine, and strength is supposed to be masculine.
>
> *Do you buy that?*
>
> No, because I've known quite a few very weak men, both emotionally and spiritually, physically, and mentally. I know many, many strong women. In fact, the majority of the women in this world have to be strong women to survive, you know. That's just the way it is.

For Roxanne, categorizing practices as masculine or feminine was merely a matter of social convention. And, for her, these conventions did not hold up under scrutiny when she compared them with her experience of men (some of whom were weak) and women (many of whom were strong). Undoubtedly, Roxanne's adolescent journey to define her sexual orientation outside fixed categories had provided her with opportunities for critical reflection on gendered meanings that many of her exclusively heterosexual peers had not experienced (not to mention her lesbian friends, who did not have boyfriends).

At the present time, of course, social agreements about gender-appropriate characteristics and behaviors are strongly contested. Women and men alike challenge the perspectives on male and female gender norms that are contained in stereotypical notions of femininity and masculinity. The very existence of female athletes challenges stereotypes of women as noncompetitive, physically weak, or soft. Men in the role of counselor or teacher challenge the stereotype that empathy and nurturing are the exclusive purview of women. In a time like ours, making sense of gender is obviously quite complex.

Joanne, for example, was from a family that had immigrated from India when she was a child. Her ways of constructing gender included the negotiation of cultural meanings in her family system as well as in her peer group, and these two sets of meanings added to the complexity of her efforts to make sense of gender.

> *What is feminine? You used that word just now—what does it mean to you?*

[Pause. Sigh.] Umm, being a lady. Like, making sure you look good at all times. Say, just being proper. [Pause.] I know it's so wrong to say, and I'm totally using stereotypes, 'cause I guess that's kind of the way—I don't know. I mean—being feminine?

Is there a difference between being female and being feminine?

Definitely. You can be female and—well, actually, maybe not. Because by saying—because being feminine is just being a girl, I mean, a lady. Being female is, you are a lady . . . I don't know. I really can't distinguish. I'm thinking, well, the best way of being feminine is wearing dresses and looking pretty—such a stereotype, because you don't have to look pretty to be female.

Girls like Joanne, sensitive to gender stereotyping, nevertheless caught themselves using what they recognized as gender typecasting in these interviews when they tried to talk about the meanings they attributed to gender differences. On the one hand, Joanne's words depict a reality that exists across much of American culture: the strong coherence between a focus on bodily appearance and the very definition of womanhood. On the other hand, her halting speech, peppered with queries and even reversals in her ideas, indicates that she began to question this previously unexamined association between being female and a particular mode of physical appearance. In midspeech, Joanne began to dissect her perspectives as inadequate to the expression of her gendered experience's full meaning.

Accommodating Bodies

Susan was among those girls who verbalized and rejected the stereotypical character of what she called "society's views" of gender. With her words, she opposed these images of gender difference:

Feminine means to be what men traditionally wanted women to be, kind of. This is my definition.

Hmm. Can you give me some examples?

I'm not even sure. When a man wanted a woman to be feminine, she had to dress nicely. She always had to be composed, and be quiet, and speak when spoken to. Umm . . . very *passive*. And that's what a man wanted a woman to be, so to be feminine now is to be what the man wants you to be, and not who you want to be. Which I don't think—I think the term feminine is to act female, and to act female is *not* necessarily to act passive. So it bothers me that I cannot be feminine and proud of it.

Even though Susan and other girls resisted social conventions of femininity in their talk about the meanings of gender, their descriptions of their own *actions* related to gender—what they did as part of being women— frequently conflicted with their ideas. That is, Susan rejected a restrictive definition of femininity defined around "what men traditionally wanted women to be." But her resistance to this definition did not translate into the ability for her to act differently, living outside the pressure to be a certain way in order to be viewed as female. For example, Susan indicated how much she was still caught up in accommodating societal perspectives on female gender in her efforts to reshape her body to be very thin. A good body, she said, would be me with a different nose and, like, forty pounds thinner. Bigger eyes and smaller cheeks, you know. Whatever society says, I guess.

Is that where your image of a good body comes from?

Yeah, but I don't think it's a male—it comes from advertising, and everyone says you have to look like this, not just males. I don't think there are very many women out there who think that you should be large and overweight to be beautiful. Maybe the men started it, but no one is helping to change it. This spring, I was going to [the beach] with . . . four of the five guys I had crushes on since I started school. And so I wanted to look good—for myself, too, a lot for myself, because I don't like the way I look. And I think I could look better. So I, uh, exercised two or three hours a day, and I didn't sleep as much as I should have . . . and I got mono . . . I actually think I'm below average now. [Laughter.]

It sounds like, though, that doesn't affect how you feel about your body—the fact that you can say, "I think I'm actually below average."

Because you can look at it [her body], and I can grab big chunks of fat off myself—obviously, it's not good enough, you know? And maybe I'm—maybe this is the way God wants me to look. But I haven't accepted that yet, and I probably never will . . . it makes me mad that I'm weak, that I cannot accept myself. And it makes me mad because I know I would look fine in a bathing suit, and the guys would like the way I look.

Girls talked about not buying into male-defined notions of womanhood or beauty. But actually living out their rejection of these gender frameworks proved very difficult for them.

Of the girls who commented directly in their interviews on feelings about their bodies, only about a third of them expressed a generally consistent sense of comfort with their bodies. Body size and weight were the problems most often named. Overwhelmingly, these girls talked about their bodies as a collection of assets and deficits, parts that they liked or wished to change.

"I try, but I still am like, 'I've got big thighs,'" lamented Ellen.

Elaine, meanwhile, expressed the double bind she experienced when male friends comment on other girls' body parts in front of her:

> Certain parts of my body I like, certain parts I don't. My thighs are too big, and I can't do anything about it.
>
> *How do you know they are too big?*
>
> Because, well, comparing—basically, society's view.
>
> *Which comes to you how?*
>
> TV, ads, et cetera. Guys. I hang out with people from youth group, we'll go to the beach or something, and they'll be making comments about girls and stuff. Like, "Oh, she looked good." Well, look, she's got the thinnest legs. [One day] they started talking about who looks good in what area. It kinda hurts, in a way, because they talk about it in front of me, which makes me feel I'm kind of special because they can talk about that kind of thing in front of me, but at the same time it's, like, they're not talking about *me*. . . . It makes me feel more self-conscious.

She went on to describe why she had difficulty articulating her image of what a "good" body would look like:

> I'm not sure [about a good body] because I'm getting confused. It used to be you need big boobs or a big butt. Now you have to be tall. You have to have some chest, but not much. You have to be very skinny. Some guys want this, others want that. Different ways, right? I guess I'm thinking again, a good body would have to be what the guys think, right? And so I don't know.

Because the standard for physical beauty is a moving target, constantly changing, girls for whom it matters to imitate this standard find themselves in the position of never arriving at the goal they seek. It also puts girls in the position of defining their body images and sexuality externally, continually rearranging their sense of physical adequacy in relation to fluctuating (male) standards of attraction.

Girls who talked about body image in their interviews frequently critiqued popular culture—music artists, TV and film stars, advertising,

Internet images—and its influences on their own body images. Yet, at least for European American girls, this *theoretical* understanding of the unrealistic effort to emulate airbrushed supermodels failed to translate into the ability to escape the tyranny of the thin and small.[2] Many, describing lifelong dislike of their bodies, made comments such as that of Michelle, who said, "I've been trying to change my body since the fourth grade." Others projected a future for themselves in such a way that it seemed they felt destined to be unhappy with their bodies for the rest of their lives:

> How I feel about my body depends on how I feel that day. In general terms, I don't like my body.
>
> *How long has that been true?*
>
> Ever since I can remember, because it has never been good enough, you know. It goes along with society, and how acceptance is based on appearance. All [those] media images that you have to change your body because the body you are given is never enough.
>
> *What would your body have to be like to be a good body, in your own opinion?*
>
> It would never. There is no ideal body for me, because I know no matter what body I would have, I wouldn't like it. There would always be something wrong with it.

Race and Gendered Bodies

Several studies of African American girls, published in the 1990s, conclude that these girls may be somewhat more immune to the self-loathing and poor body images with which their European American peers seem afflicted.[3] Similarly, the American Association of University Women's important study *Shortchanging Girls, Shortchanging America*[4] points out the apparent ability of African American girls to bring with them into adolescence the self-esteem they experienced in their elementary school years, and to hold on to that self-regard for a longer time than their white peers.

Janie Victoria Ward[5] contends that the difference lies in parenting for resistance to a racist culture. That is, African American families face the additional parenting task of "helping daughters develop healthy resistance to cultural pressures that call for maladaptive change" in dealing with race. Ward goes on to assert that for white families of adolescent girls, where traditional gender socialization and gender inequality comprise these cultural pressures, the need is to develop practices of parenting that can strengthen girls' resistance.

According to Erkut, Fields, Sing, and Marx, "For white girls, gender may indeed be the principal site for struggle and negotiation in terms of personal identity and social place. For girls of color, culturally and linguistically different girls, working-class girls, and girls living in poverty, gender is not the only site for struggle and negotiation, nor is it necessarily the most salient site."[6] Erkut and her colleagues contend that "a girl's self-regard does not develop in a social or cultural vacuum. . . . Qualities associated with 'female' in one community may not translate to 'female' in another community."[7]

Several African American girls who were my interview partners, like Nicole, supported these conclusions. They affirmed that in their communities they did not struggle to reconcile their bodies with meanings of "female" associated with a waiflike body, because other, very different meanings of girlhood and womanhood operated:

> I think at times I'm self-conscious, or whatever, about [my body] because, like, in the advertisements [they] have all the women all skinny and, like, with blond hair and eyes, and I don't have long hair at all, or blond, you know, and I know I'm not skinny. I don't think I was meant to be skinny, just because of, you know, who I am, and my family. I think that because people like you are so strong, and I'm, like, I never—I don't think I was ever meant to look like those ladies in the [advertisements]. I'm glad because I don't want to be just like that. I'm just glad I'm myself. . . . And, plus, like, black women and white women's bodies differ. Like, black women usually tend to have ample behinds and stuff like that, and it's very different. So it's hard for some people to accept that. They think that you're just fat, and you have this [problem], but actually it's part of your genetic makeup.

But even with different meanings of "female" for girls from African American communities, the power of body-conscious Anglocentric cultural perspectives to operate as norms showed up in the way some of the girls had internalized these views about appropriate female bodies, in spite of differences in their own cultural communities. For example, Mikela, an African American girl from the urban South, told this story:

> I remember, I used to go out with this boy, like, in October, and we broke up in March. I remember one time we went to a basketball game, and I said, "I wish I could lose my thighs, and I wish I had

a smaller waist." And he said, "You just described a white woman."
And I started thinking. That really made me think.

What Mikela described was a consciousness-raising experience in which
she discovered her internalizing of a European American standard of
physical beauty. She was still sorting out these perspectives at the time of
her interview, but she obviously agreed with her male date that the standards she was applying to her body were not those of her own
community.

Sometimes faith gets mingled in with ideas about the body when religious imagery appears to authorize particular bodies and not others. For
example, Brenda, another African American girl, told of internalizing
Eurocentric body norms as she described her view of God as "the white
man with the blue eyes and the hair, long hair, and white robes and
sandals":

> Well, it makes me seem inferior, that that's how people are supposed
> to look, supposed to be. You know, fair-skinned, and blue eyes and
> blond hair. And it makes me think that I'm supposed to look up to
> people that *do* have those features. Because, okay, I mean, not just
> Jesus. But if you look in a magazine, all you see is blond hair and blue
> eyes and a little nose. And a size-six figure. And sometimes that makes
> me feel ugly, that makes me feel that I'm some mistake. You know,
> that I should have been white, or I think that I'm being punished
> because I am black, you know, in a way. I'm not being prejudiced, but
> it's so much easier to make it if you are white. . . . [Being black],
> you get mistreated so many times, and, 'specially where I live. And, you
> know, you just really seem inferior to everybody else. And when
> you look at the magazines, that just makes it even worse.

For Brenda, images from popular culture (such as those in magazines)
and from common religious images (such as those seen in Sunday school
art posters) combined to underscore the idea that "how people are supposed to look" is white. Brenda's articulation of her feelings stands as a
critique of the imposition of Anglocentric body norms onto African
American girls, and as a statement of resistance in her laying bare how
religious imagery authorizes the same bodies authorized by popular
culture.

The impressions presented by the diverse voices of the girls in these
interviews offer a mixed picture of how these girls dealt with issues of
body image and self-esteem as they worked to negotiate gender identity.
On the one hand, I spoke with some girls who manifested amazing

resilience regarding body image and self-esteem. In the face of cultural norms that worked against self-acceptance and self-affirmation, these girls offered a discourse of vitality and affirmation of their bodies. On the other hand, such resilient voices were often drowned out by the words of the many girls with whom I spoke who described their bodies as "horrible" and "disgusting."

In the self-reflections of girls writing in their diaries, Brumberg finds evidence of a major shift among American girls and women that took place in the twentieth century. "Girls today," she wrote in 1998, "make the body into an all-consuming project in ways young women of the past did not."[8] Brumberg studied the diary entries of girls from the century between the 1890s and the 1990s. She contends that American girls in the 1800s, like girls today, were also concerned about improving themselves and apparently were quite thoughtful about their self-presentations to others. But when she compared the ways girls described these concerns in 1890 with how they were described by girls writing in 1990, she found a startling difference. A century ago, girls concerned with self-improvement wrote about the various character traits they hoped to acquire and display more frequently, as in this young woman's 1892 diary entry: "Resolved, not to talk about myself or feelings. To think before speaking. To work seriously. To be self restrained in conversation and actions. Not to let my thoughts wander. To be dignified. Interest myself more in others."[9] A hundred years later, Brumberg notes, girls were much more likely to be preoccupied with various desired changes to their bodies: "In the twentieth century, the body has become the central personal project of American girls. . . . Before the twentieth century, girls simply did not organize their thinking about themselves around their bodies. Today, many young girls worry about the contours of their bodies—especially shape, size, and muscle tone—because they believe that the body is the ultimate expression of the self."[10]

Many girls seemed to want to talk about gender in terms other than those involving stereotypical caricatures focused on bodily appearance, but they struggled to come up with alternatives. Girls are not the only ones struggling to find new ways to describe gendered experience. Scholars engaged in studies of gender, along with those who conduct research on human sexual behavior, are quick to point out that the very division into the two binary categories of male and female, or masculine and feminine, leads to false attributions of characteristics and behaviors as belonging exclusively either to males or to females. Such language works to foreclose the possibility that aggression and physical power, for example—traits commonly associated with men in U.S. culture—might also be modes of gender identity for girls and women.[11] Apart from the false polarity that these binary categories create, with their associated terminology, they also tend to reflect heterosexuality as the sole and normative expression of gender identity.

The process of listening to these and other girls, alongside my own experiences as a woman and as a parent of both girl and boy children, convinces me that gender is much more multiple and complex than unitary categories of male or female, boy or girl, man or woman, allow. There exists a rich tapestry of ways in which people embody and express gender, and these are informed by biology, culture, history, and social norms as well as by the varieties of sexuality present in human beings. In this way of thinking, gender difference has less to do with categorizing characteristics and behaviors as either male or female than with how differences are positioned in terms of the power and status distinctions they come to represent. Various conscious and unconscious forces work to shape the configurations and meanings of all kinds of differences, including gender differences.[12] Gender is not merely something one is born into, nor is it simply something one decides upon. It is more complex, by virtue of the fact that gender identity takes shape over time through one's participation in cultural practices, even as one may work to transform those practices along with one's identity.

Pretending to Be Less

One of the more surprising and troubling discoveries for me in these interviews came with the finding that some of the young women still willingly diminished themselves in order to fit their own notions of gender difference. For a few of the girls who spoke with me, taken-for-granted ways of framing what it meant to be female involved starting with "male" and then subtracting. If men were strong, women could be, too, only less so. If men were intelligent, so were women, but—at least at the level of appearances—they could not seem to be smarter than men, not if they wanted to be considered feminine.

Elaine, for example, invoked the language of female subservience and male control in describing masculine and feminine as opposites. Problematically, she accepted these meanings as basically inherent, natural qualities of gender difference:

> Masculine, to me, is strong, strength—not that women can't be strong, too, but masculine means *more*, more strength. More set in their ways, unchanging, in control. . . . I view masculine as what my dad is,

and feminine is more the exact opposite. It would be like weaker, more subservient, more willing to change, more accepting.

Elaine's perspective was also articulated by several other girls. What surprised me about Elaine's comment and similar remarks by other girls was how these girls appeared to be participating in their own oppression by stating beliefs about gender that support gender inequality.

Sometimes these girls simply and uncritically accepted negative understandings of female gender, as Elaine did. At other times, they seemed to collaborate in building negative meanings of female gender identity by adopting certain practices that placed males above themselves, actually or symbolically. One such practice involved girls' hiding their own intelligence in order to maintain the fiction of boys' intellectual superiority. For example, Lynn, a bright young woman of Caribbean heritage who attended an exclusive private school, spoke of seeing this practice among her friends and wondered if she should adopt it herself:

> I guess I have always questioned why I don't have a boyfriend, because I've always thought I'm a pretty friendly person, pretty approachable—you know, pretty fun. You know, sometimes I think, am I too smart? Because my friends—they play dumb. My friend [*laughter*]— she is the most intelligent person, and she plays dumb, and she has a boyfriend—that's why. But she has, like, a 4.0, you know. And she wouldn't tell him that, because . . . well.
>
> *What would happen if he knew she was smart?*
>
> Well, then he would realize, you know, that she's smarter than he is, and he feels threatened by that.

This need to ensure higher status for males seemed inconsistent with the girls' constant assertions that males were not better than they were. But somehow a number of these girls had come to understand that being a "real" girl required them to give up or downplay their own competencies in order to uphold notions of male superiority, and so they sometimes chose to diminish their own status. This process of self-diminishment could be extremely subtle; for example, sometimes it involved a symbolic marker of status difference between themselves and boys, such as height or age, that nevertheless created a gendered order between the individuals to whom this symbolic difference applied.

Why did some of these girls engage in practices to put themselves down? Among those who described self-diminishing behavior tied to gender differences, the rationale appeared to be tied up with meanings that they attributed to being female, and with their unwillingness to be "gender outlaws," girls who lived outside the boundaries of culturally prescribed femininity. Where being female means being positioned lower than males, evidence that a female is brighter, stronger, faster, taller, or more clever than a male puts her status as a woman at risk. Furthermore, the cultural perspectives on female gender that were accepted and expressed by some of these girls included the notion that being female meant being protected, and protection required a male who was larger and taller. If a girl believed that being female meant not being challenging or threatening, then she needed a male who was smarter and more able than she was, and therefore unlikely to feel challenged or threatened by her. In order to act "like girls," at least according to the standards that some of these girls had internalized, some of them were willing to diminish themselves.

By conforming to such standards, young women end up reproducing the gendered status differences between men and women that place women at the bottom of the male/female hierarchy. That is, in some sense they become the girls in their society's cultural fantasy, and in their own gendered imaginations—girls who want boys to be bigger, older, and taller, and who depend on boys to be stronger, faster, and smarter.

Jan, for example, presented herself as an assertive, powerful young woman, but her words revealed a confusing clash with her reported actions as she described shaping her sense of self around her relationships with males in ways that required her to change herself. Her accommodations to restrictive definitions of "female," over and against those of "male," resulted in a kind of "de-selfing," an abdication of her personhood:

> If I make a generalization that all guys are stronger, and I convince myself that's true, then I'd feel like if I'm stronger, then I must be more guy-like. . . . I used to think, because I had a lower voice, I feel like I had more testosterone or something, you know, because most guys have lower voices. . . . Sometimes I feel, because I have a lower voice, that makes me more masculine. I don't feel as feminine. And sometimes you kind of want to feel feminine. I kind of want to feel feminine. I guess the way I've gotten from, like, society is that the more feminine you are, sometimes the more attractive, because the guys don't want to be challenged, you know. Geez, would I feel uncomfortable— I never thought about this, but I would feel uncomfortable if my boyfriend had a higher voice than I did? . . . I'd probably feel uncomfortable dating a guy who's shorter than me—like, even though I don't think men are superior, in terms of, like, better, I know I don't

like being taller than a guy, because I would rather feel protected by
the guy. In a way, I think that's a shame.

When girls like Jan present themselves and arrange their lives in ways
that preserve illusions of male superiority, they must give up something
true about themselves ("I am stronger than some guys") in order to prop
up the myth ("All guys are stronger than girls"). Eventually they may
even come to see this myth as natural and necessary. And, as the philosopher Sandra Lee Bartky notes, this process constructs women's desire
around male dominance, in an action she calls "internal colonization" of
women's sexuality.[13] Jan "would rather feel protected by the guy"; this
becomes a condition for her desire. At the same time, her final words—
"In a way, I think that's a shame"—indicate a tragic awareness of the
false machinations involved in this process of ensuring the symbolic superiority of males.

A Changing Understanding of Girlhood

When girls talked about their understandings of gender differences, and
of masculinity and femininity, they showed the extent to which they were
caught in the crossfire of contemporary society's mixed messages about
the meanings attributed to gender. On the one hand, these girls had
received and internalized multiple versions of the fairly stereotypical and
traditional message that to be female means being quieter, softer, more
caring, and more emotional. On the other hand, they also spoke about
women and girls as having strength, ability, and power. Many actively
resisted and critiqued subordinating views of women. Their talk showed
gender to be an area still under construction.

Socially constructed understandings of gender clearly are changing.
Stereotypes that confine women and girls to certain kinds of activities no
longer hold. A girl can now dream of becoming an airline pilot or a phys-
icist or an Episcopal priest. She can play percussion instruments in her
school band without jeopardizing her fit within the gender category of
"girl." She can participate in sports and assert herself in relationships.
This new situation is good news for girls. It means that older, restrictive
understandings of girlhood are losing their ability to define girls' experiences. With the meanings of being female not exclusively bound up in
reproduction or in a certain kind of physical appearance, a girl can be
intelligent, creative, and powerful. In this spirit, a girl named Sarah spoke
of being a woman in terms of "the freedom to be and do anything. . . . I
don't have to dress a certain way or act a certain way. It's a good time to

be a girl because these days being a girl means being whatever you want."
Other girls expressed a similar sense of freedom in their interviews, defining girlhood as being without limitations.

Some girls, in fact, asserted that there are no significant differences
between males and females. Kelly, for example, said that, particularly
among teens, males and females "share the same fears and insecurities"
and are therefore not so different from one another. Joanne stated that,
beyond differences of physical adornment, there "really shouldn't be any
difference in how [girls and boys] think or act."

Abbie echoed Roxanne's sentiment that "masculinity" and "femininity" are problematic categories. She critiqued the way continued use of
these terms contributes to stereotypes, and she offered a more nuanced
understanding of the relationship between behavior and gender identity:

> To say someone is masculine just reinforces the fact that men and
> women are stereotypes. So if you use the word "masculine," are you
> saying this is kind of typical of a guy, [and] when you say that a
> woman is masculine, . . . are [you] saying that this is really weird?
> That doesn't make sense. So I try to avoid that sort of thing. I mean,
> if someone said someone was masculine, I would be, like, "That's not
> right to say that." I mean, words are words, you know, but if you
> want to get fussy about how you say things, then I would definitely
> say avoid using those, and just explain it as it is. Crying is considered
> feminine. I prefer to say it's *sensitive* rather than feminine, you know,
> and it is. It just puts it in a more neutral sense, and it's okay for a guy
> to cry. And to say that guy is acting feminine—it puts a negative judg-
> ment on the act as a whole, and it just sounds stupid, you know.

Similarly, Leslie was in the process of reframing her perspectives on
gender difference. She believed that there are some features of identity
unique to women but was beginning to shift from viewing those distinctions as "natural" and to seeing them instead as products of women's
positioning in the larger society, features shared by other groups in subordinate positions:

> I think the way we [women and girls] look at life and the world are
> unique. Because we are a minority looking at things, and kind of on
> the bottom. I think that is unique—our position. But at the same time,
> I don't think it's totally unique to women. I think it is something that
> minorities share. Who you are, how you look at life, as far as gender—
> that does influence things. But I think that other factors can influence
> in similar ways—maybe race or poverty or things like that.

Leslie was self-conscious and intentional about her efforts to reconsider gender roles:

> I've been trying hard to break down the stereotypes of men and women. I think things like compassion, like love and caring, are thought of as feminine, and strength and power and those things are thought of as masculine. But I think that's very limiting. I don't think traits or characteristics should be classified as that, because anyone can be caring, or anyone can have strength. It bothers me. . . . [Getting rid of notions of masculine and feminine] would be a lot more fair. Then people would feel more free to be who they are, and who God created them to be.

Here, Leslie was speaking of a sense in which people, conforming to gender-role stereotypes, live their lives as people other than the ones "God created them to be." She and many other girls grasped the fact that common uses of the term "feminine" often contain implicit references to lesser power, status, competence, and importance. Jan stated this idea quite directly:

> Feminine . . . umm, I guess that's the things you don't take real seriously. Umm, stuff that doesn't really have a lot to do with, like, power, you know—having strength, you know. Stuff that would more, like, make you, you know, give a laugh—you know, more entertaining stuff than real, like, serious stuff.

Asked if she thought of this characterization as a stereotype, or if she saw it as a true depiction of women, Jan said, "It's both. It's society's stereotype of women. But it also has something true about it." Jan's perception highlights the complexity of negotiating what gender means in a girl's developing sense of herself. On the one hand, most of these girls recognized that they did not need to limit who they were to gender-based stereotypes. On the other hand, some, like Jan, recognized that sometimes there did seem to be a match between the stereotypes and their own experiences as girls, regardless of whether they attributed this match to the sexism in society that shapes female gender roles or to something "essential" about being female that gets expressed in stereotypes about women. In either case, the meaning of being a girl today is not a simple one that can be taken for granted.

The concomitant mixture of freedom and closure around meanings of gender constitutes a mixed message to girls about the meaning of gender in contemporary society. In fact, at the very same time that newer, freer understandings of what it means to be a girl are taking shape in our society, some analysts note a contemporary move to reimpose notions of women's subordination onto current notions of girlhood and femininity. A newly released report by a task force of the American Psychological Association points to a trend that affects girls at increasingly younger ages: the sexualizing of their clothing and appearance, a trend driven by marketing and by media images that depict girls as sexually alluring.[14] This report is appropriately critical of the effects of such early sexualization on girls' body images and self-esteem. It critiques the forces that orient girls, from a very young age, toward "looking good" for others. I am reminded of an advertising campaign that was launched during my own adolescence, in which old-fashioned black-and-white photographs of women being reprimanded for smoking were juxtaposed with full-color photographs of modern, "liberated" women blatantly enjoying their cigarettes in public. Women, as these ads put it, may have "come a long way," but the gains of that kind of "progress" were dubious, at best, and the mixed message was confusing and troubling. Likewise, in a society in which being female is virtually synonymous with being sexy, adolescent girls trying to shore up their membership in the group known as women may well engage in the display of hypersexualized, ultimately self-undermining behavior.

Like Jan's words on femininity, this report on the sexualization of girls is a crucial reminder that notions of "girlhood without limits" are probably naive. They fail to take account of the various social forces still at work, visibly and invisibly, to limit girls' choices and opportunities, shaping the meanings of girlhood in narrow ways that then come to be seen as natural and necessary to the very definition of being female. For example, even though girls may develop their skills in math and the sciences, and even though they are free to choose education and careers in these areas, the actual number of young adult women entering the sciences and engineering remains small, a fact frequently attributed to females' being less "naturally" able in math and science. To take another example, girls in the Roman Catholic tradition of Christianity may well dream of being religious leaders in their church, but they are not yet free to seek the vocation of priesthood in their faith communities. And women remain far more likely to work for large corporations than to head them. Thus it is simply not true that all gender barriers have been lifted, and that the sky is the limit for girls today.

At the same time, however, some barriers have been lifted for some girls. Definitions of girlhood actually are in the process of changing. It has never been more imperative for adults who care about the thriving of girls to participate in this change process.

Family Gender Messages

In talking about gender, girls in the interviews often referred to the messages they had received from their parents. In implicit ways, too, by observing the gender roles enacted by family members, girls internalized certain expectations for women. For example, Jessica spoke of gendered divisions of labor in her family that had shaped her understanding of men's and women's roles:

> First of all, I'm very proud of being a woman. I do think they're supposed to be—I think—I see them as kind of the head of the family, emotionally. Like, the man is the head of the family in the money area, you know. I still have that family structure. But, umm, the woman kind of holds it together. I'm kind of proud of—I like that.

> *How come it's like that?*

> I don't know. She has the children, she takes care of them. I don't know. [*Laughter.*] She is—the woman is seen as the more loving type [of] person. I think we show our emotions more. I'm not saying that men are less loving. . . . The only difference, you know—the men being the stronger ones. I don't know. A lot of times, it seems like they have it more together. Maybe not—I don't know! [*Laughter.*]

> *You look kind of puzzled about all of this.*

> Yeah, I am! [*Laughter.*] Because, I mean—I don't know. I was thinking the woman is strong, like, with her children. She is the one who will raise them. I don't know a major difference. I don't think there's that much difference besides the anatomy, the hormones—we're all basically just people.

Jessica ended up saying, "We're all basically just people," yet her pride about being a woman was grounded in a male-female division of labor in her family, with women assuming emotional leadership. At the time of her interview, she had no critical perspective on this division, speaking as if she assumed that the roles she had observed in her parents were universal, and therefore natural features of gender difference.

Similarly, Andrea expressed uncritical acceptance of the gendered role divisions she observed in her parents, to which she added her perspective that it is God who underwrites and authorizes such arrangements:

> My mom, well—she's her own person, and she can still make her own decisions, but yet he [my dad] is still the ultimate [authority]. . . . I mean, maybe that's how I grew up, but that's just how it is—the

man-is-the-head-of-the-household type of thing. To me, that means comfort. I mean, to me it's, like, God and then, like, my husband. I need to submit to my husband—to God first, and then to my husband when I get married.

Okay, I understand what you're saying about an order. But I'm trying to understand what it means to submit to your husband in that situation. What exactly does that mean?

I don't know. Like, I just think that there needs to be a figure in the household that's like—like with my parents, my dad does not dominate or control my mom, but he's still the ultimate authority in our house. I think that's just part of life. I mean, someone needs to be the ultimate authority, to be in charge, to tell you what to do, in a sense—not really, but kind of. To guide you. And I think the man needs to almost guide the woman. Not that [the] woman's lower. Unless—I just think that's how God made it.

Here, Andrea took the arrangement observed in her own household and universalized it, seeing it as divinely arranged—and presumably, therefore, a necessary given in relations between women and men. She was working out an understanding of how gender situates women and men in relation to one another, in conjunction with viewpoints appropriated from her religious tradition that draw on the specific language of wives needing to "submit" to their husbands (see Ephesians 5:22).

Other girls, however, did take a more critical view of their parents' practices in relation to gender roles at home. Jan said:

Like, I wouldn't say that they made me feel inferior, but I definitely feel stereotypes coming from my parents, you know—I guess from my father right now. I think there are fathers that make their daughters feel, like—you know, like, double standards. And that's true, 'cause I get that a lot 'cause of differences in the sexes. They discriminate between my brother and I sometimes.

Occasionally these young women also heard direct talk about gender from their parents. Mikela spoke of the women in her family holding different expectations for women than for men:

Well, like, now, from my mother sometimes, when she's talking to my aunts, and they're talking about women. They were talking about a lady who has a child by my uncle, but they are not married, and she's kind of wild. She takes care of my cousin, but she doesn't really do a good job of it. And when my mother and them talk about her and stuff, they expect more out of her than they do of my uncle. And I think he should be—that he should take responsibility, too, sometimes. I mean, he does, but they don't really say it. They say she should be at home with that child, and it's like a double standard. And I don't think that's right. And when different women—like, say, if a woman does something, then they'll say it's okay for a man, but not for a woman, and stuff like that—different situations. I haven't really gotten any negative messages—a lot of double standards.

But some girls heard gender talk or observed practices at home that invited them to challenge unfair treatment of women. Kit recalled

a time I was in the kitchen helping with dinner, and on NPR [National Public Radio] news there was a report about women working two jobs, one at their offices and then one at home. And my mom and dad got into a big discussion about whether that happens to her. And they both agreed it wasn't fair. Right then and there, they figured out that she was carrying more of the load at home. So we kind of rejuggled things to make it more equal. That's pretty much what I grew up with. It's never perfect, but they both try to pay attention to whether they are doing things just because that's a job for women, or for men, instead of out of what's fair.

Some girls conveyed a strong sense of the distance between their situations and those of their mothers. On the one hand, this gap posed a problem, best summed up by Laura:

My mother is totally and completely clueless when it comes to anything about being female today. It is like she was born on another planet. I mean, in her family, girls really didn't even get much education. They were just expected to marry and have babies. That's the last thing on my mind. My mother cannot even fathom that I would go out with a guy I don't have any intention of "getting serious" with, because for her the whole reason to date was to find a husband. I'm not looking for a husband—not anytime soon.

On the other hand, girls who were attuned to the gap between their mothers' experience as women and their own experience also spoke with gratitude about the differences between their two eras of being women:

My mom tells me stuff from when she was younger, about how certain things were forbidden because they were unladylike. I don't think anyone would ever tell me not to do something by reason of it being unladylike. I'm glad I don't have to put up with that!

Recalling my own mother's explanation of why she never learned to ride a bike or whistle, and why she was not expected to go to college or use a hammer—"These things weren't ladylike"—I, too, feel a sense of gratitude at the changing tide of gender norms as well as a lingering awareness that, like my mother before me, I also stand embedded in an era that limits what is possible, in ways that I cannot now see or know, but that surely my own daughter will recognize.

Faith and Gender Identity in Girl Talk

Girl talk on gender often overlapped with girl talk on faith. Several of the examples just cited show girls and their families engaging religious faith as a worldview in which women's roles are subordinate, more circumscribed, and more limited than those of men. And a number of girls described dissonance between their personal beliefs about gender differences and practices of religious communities that failed to authorize the full participation or leadership of women and girls. Most girls remarking on such dissonant intersections were highly critical of their religious communities for promoting inequality between women and men, even while they continued to see themselves as belonging to their faith communities.

Abbie, for instance, came from a Roman Catholic family and church. She was agitated as she explained, "I don't like what it means to be a woman in my church":

> Women are inferior there. I can remember there were—in sixth grade, there were no boys that wanted to be altar boys. All the girls wanted to, and the lady who was the coordinator for this said, "No, you are not allowed," and we all were "Why? Why?" And she couldn't answer it, she couldn't answer. So the father [priest] said, "I don't want any girls." And that was, like, the first blow, and I was, like, what is this? This is not fair, this is not right, and in everything else I've been equal.

For Nicole, the dissonance showed up at Sunday school, in the form of a double standard for girls and boys regarding sexual activity:

> When I was in Sunday school, this guy who was the teacher was telling us—he was, like, it was against the Bible, it's against the rule of the Bible, to commit fornication. He was mainly talking to the girls, not even to the guys in the class. It was, like, the only thing you could probably do is kiss a person on the cheek, or a handshake, all of this stuff, but he wasn't talking to the guys. So we were like, why are you telling *us* this, we probably have more sense about it than they do!

Roxanne levied her critique against "traditional religion" in contrast to her own beliefs and those of her religious community:

> Traditionally, religion teaches that women are second to men. Like, men can be anything—they can be teachers, they could be ministers, they can be servants, they can be street sweepers. You know, they can be anything, but women can only be what men choose *not* to be, so if a man chose to be a teacher instead of a street sweeper, then the women have to take the leftover—have to take the street sweeper, you know, but women could never be teachers or preachers or important people, because men would always choose to be important people instead of being unimportant people. That's definitely not my view. I believe that everyone has the authority and potential and right to be a teacher or preacher or a server because God loves all of us, and so we all have the right to share what God's love means to us.

Brenda expressed a mixed perspective on her faith community's views concerning women. On the one hand, she critiqued the idea of male superiority. On the other hand, seeing this perspective grounded in a Biblical authority that she was not prepared to critique, she simultaneously voiced acceptance "up to an extent":

> You know, as a woman, you're expected to be submissive to a guy, and submissive to society. And in Biblical terms, I think you should be, up to an extent. But I really resent that. Just because I'm a woman doesn't mean a guy is any better than me or has authority over me. And so I have a problem with God wanting me to, you know, "honor thy husband," and "man shall rule over you," and stuff.
>
> *Do you think God wants you to be submissive—is that what you mean?*
>
> To a certain extent, I think He does.
>
> *Does your church have any particular teachings about women?*
>
> Yeah, they teach that women should be—"the man shall have rule over thee; the women shall not be outspoken," they should not be an embarrassment.

The problem, of course, was that Brenda did not act like a sidekick, so she had to find ways to reconcile her outspokenness with her religiously informed notions about being female. She seemed to do this in part by selecting certain arenas (school, extracurricular activities) in which to assert her strength and competence, leaving other arenas (her religious participation, and perhaps her relationships with boyfriends) as places for greater conformity with such notions of women as submissive to men. The fact that Brenda raised objections ("I have a problem with God wanting me to . . .") to the religious perspectives on male-female relationships that had been a part of her upbringing signaled a significant moment of resistance to a set of meanings that clashed with something Brenda knew about herself as a female: "Just because I'm a woman doesn't mean a guy is any better than me or has authority over me."

Many of the experts—psychologists, sociologists, educators—who study women and girls would have us believe that the only role of religious communities in the lives of girls and women is a problematic one of encouraging women's subordination. For the majority of the girls with whom I spoke, however, Christian faith operated in at least some aspect to authorize the transformation of oppressive gender arrangements, and to support women's empowerment. This was particularly true in instances where girls saw women's empowerment modeled in their congregations. Leslie, for example, spoke of a minister who was a role model for her:

> At our church, we had an interim minister for the past year and a half. She was really a model to me because she was only working part-time at the time but was also a wife and a mother, and she balanced every—at least tried to balance everything. And that was a real model for me because I've always felt like I want to get married and have kids, but I also want a career. And I think watching this individual being able to do both was really inspiring to me. There've been other women I've met through the church—a couple of teachers, some really neat people—showing by their example what women can be and do.

Girls spoke of women in their congregations, clergy as well as laity, who modeled for them what it meant to be a good person and a good woman. Leslie included her mother and her minister in describing her images of good women:

> There's a lot of women that I know who I think are good women . . . like my mom. But I also think of other people—like, the minister at our church is a good woman. I think a good woman—she's committed to something. My mom was always real committed to us as a family and totally was there—and [good women] believe in themselves and what they are doing. And they believe in God and in the saving power of God. To me, Christianity is very important. Someone who is committed and who cares about others is a good woman.

Such perspectives were underscored in many of these interviews, in which girls said that their faith communities and traditions were sources of affirmation for what was good about being a girl.

Roxanne spoke about "sifting out the problematic messages that society gives about being Christian and female, to focus on what is more at the core of faith—that God made and loved people in all their differences, including women."

Althea said that her church was "not always so good on women's issues" but attributed that shortcoming more to the people in her church than to Christianity: "Christianity is good on women because Jesus was."

And Leslie, describing the messages her faith community had given her about being female, concluded:

> I think, in talking about being a woman, that it's hard, and I don't feel it'll ever be easy, because there's things that we as women do, like having kids and stuff, that men will never understand. But I also think it's wonderful. I would never change that about myself if I could. It's too wonderful to change.

Ultimately, these girls did not separate who they were as girls and who they were as Christians. Their gender identities and religious lives took shape in relation to each other, mutually informing and transforming each other. This finding suggests that it matters greatly what kinds of raw materials girls are able to draw on in their active construction of gendered and religious selfhood. One way to support the religious lives of girls, then, is to participate with them in faith communities where women and men hold leadership roles of various kinds, where girls see themselves in stories and models of faithful living, where adults and youth engage in critical reflection on the uses of sacred texts and religious authority with respect to gender norms, and where there is support for girls to try on roles "outside the box" of socially proscribed gender identity.

Reflections

Negotiating gender—its meanings, roles, practices, and power relations—is extremely hard work. And there are no clear templates, no prefabricated designs, providing safe and foolproof paths for adolescent girls today as they sort out the meanings of girlhood and womanhood. For developmental and cultural reasons, gender matters take on heightened significance in adolescence. At the same time, however, there are also too few places for girls today to explore out loud, with others, the emotional, social, and religious meanings of gender. This means that too many girls are being left to sort out these important matters on their own, in isolation.

For me, talking with girls about their perspectives on gender brought to mind again how exciting and difficult my own experience in adolescence had been when it came to sorting out the meanings of being female. It also caused me to wonder again about the relationship between girl talk and God talk in the lives of girls. Christians have no single way of understanding gender and gender differences; in fact, Christian tradition and practice offer multiple examples of contradictory perspectives on gender. It is also true that Christianity, across many geographical contexts and across many centuries, stands implicated in the oppression of women. This contradictory and problematic history raises important questions. Where in the Christian tradition might one look for a theological perspective on gender that can support the thriving of adolescent girls? And why would one look to the Christian tradition for such a perspective?

The question of why one might look to Christianity is especially important. As noted earlier, some people, among them scholars in psychology as well as some feminist scholars of religion, believe that Christianity's record with women is so hopelessly tarnished that it would be useless to look to this faith tradition for perspectives that can support women's well-being. The fact that churches continue to structure their institutional lives and leadership in patriarchal ways that subordinate women is for these scholars reason enough to turn away from Christianity as a resource for women and girls today. Likewise, they consider the history of Christian theology, with its sometimes blatantly negative views of women, too ambivalent about gender for Christianity to be a viable spiritual path that affirms women and their experiences. Why, then, in the face of such critiques, do I continue to understand Christianity as a way of life that upholds women and contributes to their thriving?

As a feminist theologian, a minister, and a woman seeking in my own life to walk in the ways of Jesus, I continue to look for light and truth in the Christian tradition. I do so because of my conviction that the central focus of this faith, which has been distorted by sexism but cannot be rubbed out completely, is the good news inaugurated by Jesus' life—that God is at work to renew and restore all of creation to God's vision of love and justice. That vision includes the lives of girls and women. Some of the girls interviewed for this book did lack critical perspective on certain ideas and practices in their faith communities, practices that upheld gender inequality; overall, however, these girls were strategic interpreters of their religious traditions, able to recognize and work around problematic messages about women's subordination, and to lay claim to the many helpful ways their faith traditions affirmed and supported them in a vital way of life.

Christianity is a vision of the kind of life God means for God's people and creation to have, a life in which there is an end to suffering and oppression. The girls in these interviews grasped that vision whenever they talked about vocation and ways to offer their lives for the repair of the world. Scripture tells us that in this vision of life, wherein Christians imagine God's desires for the flourishing of humanity, "the blind see, the deaf hear, the lame walk, and the prisoners go free" (see Luke 4:18; Isaiah 61:1). Here, the everyday work of Christians is to care for the "widows and orphans" of our time, those people at the margins of society and at the bottom of its power hierarchies, which are themselves often defined by oppressive gender roles.

This vision finds expression in Bible stories and in the lives of Christians throughout the ages who have sought to live their faith every day. In written and lived embodiments of faith, those who are poor are lifted up, and it is children and youth, rather than those who have power in the world, who offer the best clues to understanding what matters to the heart of God. In the vision for God's creation that lies at the heart of Christianity, people who are strangers to one another, people with all kinds of differences, including gender differences, will come from east and west, north and south, and sit together *in all their differences* at God's banquet table. All will be welcome there; all will be fed, and no one will go away hungry. This Christian vision of hope and new possibility for human lives, relationships, and even institutions to be transformed is what lies beneath my ongoing search within Christianity for theological perspectives that enhance the well-being of girls and women. These girls—emerging critical interpreters of the Christian tradition who are also working to redefine what it means to be female—increase my sense of hope.

4

GIRL TALK ON MOTHERS

_____

SEVERAL YEARS AGO, while working as a clinical social worker in a teen medical clinic, I had the opportunity to meet a lively mother-daughter pair who were struggling in their relationship. They had come to the clinic seeking help with the conflicts they were having as they each adjusted to the daughter's newly diagnosed diabetes. In the course of one of our meetings, the mother lamented the fact that she felt so much distance in their relationship, compared to the days when her daughter was in elementary school.

"I hardly know my daughter anymore," she told me sadly. "And we used to be so close." She turned to her daughter. "We talked every day, about anything. I knew what you cared about, what excited you, which friend hurt your feelings that day. We sat together in church on Sundays. Now I never see you, and when I am with you, you're always mad at me. I miss you," she said mournfully.

"No, you don't," her daughter replied, voice edged with anger. "You miss who I used to be. The person I am now, you haven't even gotten to know, so how could you miss me? I'm not the same, not at all, and you just don't understand. You want me to be someone I'm not anymore! You think the important thing is to sit together in church. Meanwhile, I've given my heart to God, and I'm way past just sitting in church. You don't even know me."

The mother looked hurt and baffled. She remained silent for a few minutes. Then she said, "Déjà vu—I had this same conversation with my mother when I was sixteen. I remember feeling like she didn't want me to grow up, like she was trying to keep me as her little girl all my life, when I was bursting to get out and live my own life. And at some point, I remember feeling so unsatisfied with her just-sitting-there faith that I went off and joined this group of Christian kids protesting against the

Vietnam War. I thought that faith had to mean something in real life, or it was just going through the motions. And my mother didn't seem to understand that at all. I was ready to live, and I felt like my mom kept trying to protect me from life."

At that, the daughter's eyes teared up.

"You," she said to her mother, "protesting against the war? Wow, Mom, I never knew that about you. Was Grandma really overprotective? That's exactly how I feel about you. See, Mom? You are the only one who really understands me right now."

The mother glanced at her daughter with a tired sigh. "Can both of these things be true at the same time? I don't even know you, but I'm the only one who understands you right now? There's no logic to this relationship anymore!"

This conversation expresses what many other mothers and daughters have felt or said in their own words: the relationship between mother and daughter is shifting terrain during a girl's adolescence, but even in the midst of these shifts, the relationship remains tremendously important for both. Often such relational shifts seem to defy logic and cannot easily be explained. Nevertheless, many theorists have tried to explain the intensity and emotional valence of mothers and daughters, naming everything from hormonal changes to separation anxiety, in their efforts to make sense of this relationship's volatility. At the same time, not many theorists have attended to the role that adolescent faith has in reshaping mother-daughter relationships, or to the possibility that mothers influence the religious lives of their daughters. This chapter looks at mother-daughter relationships through the window of girls' conversations about their mothers and faith.

Good News About Mothers and Daughters

The mother-daughter relationship is a subject for film, fiction, poetry, and popular psychology in North America, where its meanings and significance are shaped by a cultural fantasy (in addition to whatever personal circumstances surround a particular mother-daughter pair). That is, North American society is heavily laden with expectations about the mother-daughter relationship as embodying a special kind of connection.

And there is some evidence to show that this is not just a fantasy. Girls report having strong bonds with their mothers across adolescence and relying on that relationship to support and shape their identities. Other research underscores a unique emotional intensity and special level of identification in the mother-daughter relationship. Whether their connection is harmonious, conflicted, or mixed in emotional tenor, mothers and daughters impute special qualities of connection to their relationship. Also supporting and enhancing this quality is another cultural fantasy: that of the mother-daughter relationship as a bond between two generations of females, a bond different from that in any other relationship. Studies of the psychology of girls and women underscore the centrality of relational connections in their lives, beginning with and perhaps rooted in the relationship a girl has with her mother.

In recent years, however, another cultural fantasy has sprung up alongside these expectations for a special bond in the mother-daughter relationship. This newer fantasy depicts adolescent girls as inevitably disturbed and under siege, psychologically if not physically. Within the last decade, a flurry of research and writing, scholarly as well as popular, has put adolescent girls on the map, so to speak, of social concern in the United States, alerting us to the reality that all is not well with girls. This literature makes clear that girls struggle with body image, with safety, and with an educational system that renders them invisible. They must deal with pernicious dynamics of inclusion, exclusion, and bullying in relationships with other girls. They are stressed by forced choices between relationships in which they have competing loyalties; for example, does spending time with a boyfriend take priority over spending time with other girls? Not only must an adolescent girl face the developmental task of identity formation, which concerns the match between her internal sense of self and the self she presents to others, she must also, in many cases, deal with the connections and disconnections between her "real" and "virtual" self-presentations as she navigates the online relational networks that are increasingly significant for girls. This is a hard time, we are told, to be an adolescent girl.

Along with countless other mothers of girls, I greet this literature on girls with a divided heart and mind. On the one hand, these books and studies are much needed, and they bring welcome attention to the particularity of girls coming into adolescence today. Such writing shines a spotlight on the special stressors and difficulties inherent in girls' lives as they stand caught between old, stereotypical gender norms, which still shape cultural fantasies of what it means to be a girl, and new possibilities, which construct girlhood around entirely different markers. As a mother, and as a professional woman who has devoted significant energy to advocacy for girls, I am grateful for research and writing that allow educators and public policymakers to see and act on the reality that girls are being harassed in school hallways and socialized into impossible expectations for what constitutes an acceptable body. On the other hand, I share with many other mothers of girls a sense of alarm, discouragement, and concern about the negative characterizations of adolescent girls *and their mothers* that have grown out of these studies of girls today. When Mary Bray Pipher describes adolescent girls as Ophelias who lose confidence in themselves, drowning in a pool of depression, stress, and pain, her depiction rings true in my experience with some girls, and yet the only advice she seems to have for the mothers of girls is to expect that struggle and conflict will be inevitable in our relationships with our daughters.[1] And Lyn Mikel Brown's excellent book *Girlfighting* ends with a long, overwhelming list of things that I, as a mother, need to be doing in order to contribute to my daughter's resilience in the face of relational problems among girls.[2] Adolescent girls need so much, and I, a mere mortal, have no doubt that I am not up to the task. And so, as I began writing this chapter, I found myself worrying that I might inadvertently contribute to what is already a thick layer of maternal anxiety. I do not want "Support for the religious life of your adolescent daughter" to become one more item on the checklist of all the things that we mothers are supposed to do to help steer our daughters through rocky shoals.

But reading once more through the transcripts of my interviews with girls helped me let go of this concern. What stood out for me were four bits of good news about the religious lives of girls, and these are relevant to mothers' involvement:

1. Just as girls construct their sense of self or identity relationally, so also do they develop their religious identities in engagement with the various relationships in their lives. Since a girl's relationship with her mother remains one of the most significant among these, there is a sense in which she engages in a kind of de facto use of her relationship with her mother to form and support her religious life. To put this idea differently, even when a mother is not trying to contribute to the spiritual life of her daughter, she may well be doing so, because her daughter, as an agent in her own growth, uses all the available relational resources in her context, in all sorts of ways. Although I believe that it does help if a girl's mother and father are intentional in their efforts to support the religious life of their daughters, it is certainly the case that, even without intending to, parents still may play a silent role in nurturing a daughter's spirituality.

2. Because girls' religious lives develop and take place relationally, a variety of other people, especially other women, also contribute to

girls' spiritual thriving. Everything does not depend on mothers. My friend and coauthor Dori Grinenko Baker has several friends with preteen daughters, and she tells me that her friends are intentionally setting her up to be in relationships with their daughters so that when the girls become adolescents, they will already have a connection with an adult woman, not their parent, who can participate in supporting their developing spiritual lives. The "other mother" in African American contexts—a woman who takes a maternal interest and role in a girl's life, apart from the girl's relationship with her biological mother—is another example of how an adult woman can contribute to the religious life of a girl. The retrieval and redevelopment of the Christian concept of godparents has a similar place in reminding mothers that, although much depends on us, we are not alone in parenting our daughters and supporting their religious lives.

3. Listening to the theological perspectives shared by these girls reminded me of an important core affirmation from my tradition within Christian theology: no human being can cause another person to have faith. Faith ultimately comes to us as a gift from God. Mothers who care about the religious lives of their daughters may certainly act to encourage religious practices and to value spirituality in their homes, in ways that promote receptivity or openness to faith. They may apprentice their daughters in certain religious practices, communicate and pass on core values and commitments, and make a variety of choices designed to encourage spiritual wholeness and growth in their daughters. But ultimately it is God who gives faith; girls embody and enact it in their own lives. This affirmation represents an opportunity, then, for mothers to participate with God in God's work of cultivating the spiritual flourishing of girls; it does not simply constitute one more item in a checklist of demands on mothers.

4. In their conversations on mothers and faith, these girls reminded me that conflict happens at some point in most meaningful and strong relationships, including those of mothers and daughters. What these girls suggested as they described their relationships with their mothers is that these relationships included points of positive connection and points of conflict or disharmony, both of which could operate in the service of facilitating the religious life of a girl in adolescence. Because so many popular associations exist between the concept of spirituality and notions of peace, harmony, and goodwill, it would

be easy for a mother to think that the only time she contributes to her daughter's religious life is when conflict, disagreement, or struggle is absent. But these girls indicated that at many points they had experienced important growth in their religious lives and practices precisely in and from the challenges that had come out of their greatest struggles with their mothers.

What Makes a Good Mother?

When girls talk about their mothers, they are never just talking about their mothers alone. They are inevitably also talking about the cultural fantasy of motherhood—an image of the Good Mother that has been shaped by often invisible or unconscious cultural perspectives. As a result, when I asked girls to describe their ideas of a good mother, I got to hear a lot about mothers baking cookies and daughters taking homemade cupcakes to school for birthday celebrations, mothers sewing the perfect Halloween costume and daughters being tucked in at night. Ironically, most of these images of good mothering came from an earlier time in the mother-daughter relationship, before adolescence.

Beyond these domestic fantasies of motherhood, filled in as they were by stereotypical feminine-role depictions, the girls seemed intent on conveying the idea that a good mother is one who is "there for" her daughter. This idea flies in the face of the cultural image of adolescent girls defecting from their relationships with their mothers. Ellen, for example, whose mother's neurological illness limited her mobility, began her description of a good mother with stereotypical images of cooking and sewing before she summarized her meaning in different terms:

> Oh, well, just that unconditional love—so sacrificing, too, just, like—willing to give up for, you know. And always there, real caring—really cares about you. And I've learned that it doesn't matter whether or not they cook and [*laughter*] do all that stuff. But it's, uh, the small things, kind of the love and all, that they show for you. So . . . I really admire my mom, though. She's been so strong through her problems. She's not let down at all. She's not given up at all. She keeps trying every single day. I mean, she does not let up. And it's amazing. I don't see how she does it. It would get so lonely being in a house by yourself. I mean, it would be for me. I would go crazy. Because just think that she used to do everything that we are doing. And now she can't.

For Ellen, the experience of her mother's fortitude and courage in the face of physical limits created an opportunity for reflection on the meanings she attached to good mothering. She realized that "it doesn't matter whether or not they cook." What mattered to Ellen was the love she felt for and from her mother, and the example of strength in the face of adversity that her mother offered every day.

In numerous interviews, girls spoke about their mothers as models and examples of integrity and faith. Many girls, for example, when I asked them to identify people they thought of as models of a good woman or a mature person of faith, named their mothers. Here is Nadine:

> My mom—she is my hero, or I guess I really should say my heroine. [*Laughter*.] If I tried hard, I would not be able to think of someone better who shows me what being a good woman looks like.

> *In what ways does she do that for you?*

> My mom—she is the same on the inside as she is on the outside. What she believes is how she acts. And what she believes in is not living for herself only, or trying to make lots of money to buy more things. She is all about caring for the children in her [special education] classroom. To her, that's straight from Jesus. I know, because sometimes we talk about how she ended up being a teacher, and why she keeps with it when it is so hard sometimes. She says it's about walking in faith. My mom is a great example of a good woman.

Similarly, Sarah held her mother in great esteem. Her mother played a key role in exemplifying the unselfish love that Sarah understood as being what the love of God is also like:

> I think the meaning of life is to love everybody. And I think it's easier to do that if you have a sense that God loves everybody as much as He loves you, and that we're all somewhat similar in certain ways, or that we all have the basic—well, we're all human.

> *What is that love, for you, if you were to describe it?*

> Well, I consider it like a relationship—the relationships I have where I love people . . . um, I would say that they're honest. I guess I'll just say like my relationship with my mom. I feel like I can tell her anything. And I know she might not always agree with everything, and she might disapprove and be disappointed, but she won't ever stop loving me. And so I think honesty has a big thing to do with love. I also think—I don't know if "sacrifice" is the right word, but "unselfishness."

It is interesting to note the close connection between the qualities that girls like Sarah associated with divine love and those they associated with their mothers. Perhaps psychoanalysts from the so-called object relations school got it right when they theorized that our most basic capacities for imagining and relating to the Holy take shape out of what Daniel N. Stern calls "the first relationship,"[3] the connection of an infant with a primary caregiver, usually a mother. In adolescence, girls remap their relationships with their mothers as well as their relationships with God. What girls like Sarah help us to know is how deeply mother love continues to resonate in girls' reconfiguring of their adolescent understandings of God.

Supporting Daughters by Having a Life

As a person born toward the end of the baby boom, I belong to a generation of women who expected to have jobs or careers as well as families. Many of my women friends and associates now struggle mightily over the conflicts they feel around juggling work and family, particularly when cultural fantasies of the Good Mother remain so active in the collective psyche (and in public policymakers' actions). It may be a product of my working-class background, or it may be that I am oddly wired in relation to how I love my work in addition to loving my children; but, for whatever reason, I have never felt that working makes me a bad mother.

In fact, I contend that my work is one of the primary ways in which I care for my children, in terms of concrete support (food on the table, a roof over our heads, money to buy shoes) and in terms of what it means about who I am as a person. My work constitutes a principal avenue for living out my vocation (my calling from God to use my gifts in service to others). Therefore, when I am engaged in purposive, meaningful work, I model for my children, and especially for my daughter, an important aspect of religious life: that of shaping one's life around passionate, engaged forms of offering one's gifts in an effort to make a difference in the world.

Girls spoke often in their interviews about their mothers' work as a source of pride and inspiration. Sarah, for example, reflecting on her mother's work in a nonprofit care facility for people with disabilities, spoke of the admiration she felt for her mother. Her mother had started out providing direct physical care to the residents of that facility. Over time, she had put herself through school and eventually became the director of personnel:

> Throughout the years, she has just stayed there because she likes her job. . . . My mom is one of my heroes. I really admire her. . . . I mean, there are a lot of things about her I don't like, necessarily, but she and

my grandma are both very giving. My mom doesn't get paid very much, but she still works at her job because she likes the fact of what she's doing.

Sarah, inspired by her mother's work, also admired her aunt, who had joined the Peace Corps and ended up making that her life's work:

I don't know if I want to make a living out of it like my aunt did, but I'd at least like to do that. I really think service is important. I know everyone has their own calling, but I think that, for me, it's really in the area of service. I feel like everyone's responsible to help change systems of oppression or chaos, and I feel like the way I could help do that is through service.

Similarly, Laura spoke of admiring her mother because her mother offered her a model for overcoming obstacles in order to do the kind of work she wanted to do:

Yes, she's a very strong person, and I admire her a lot because she lived in—she was born in Belize, and she went to college there, and then she came here, and she had to go to college again, and she is a straight-A student, and she is still in school now, to become an administrator. She doesn't stop, she just keeps going until she reaches the highest—the highest possible level that she can be. So I really admire her, and she keeps pushing and encouraging me the same way, so I admire her. That's the way I want to be. My mother—she is very strong. She's intelligent, and she speaks her mind about whatever it is, no matter what. She will let you know. If you are doing something wrong, she lets you know, no matter who it is.

When a mother evidences her strengths and passions in life, including her work life, she offers support for her daughter to view herself as a strong, passionate young woman.

Lynn commented on her mother's sense of vocation, which combined child care with a career:

I don't have anything against children. I love children, and I want to have children some day. But it's, like, I'm not ready right now. And I don't know when I'll be ready, but when I am, I think I'm going to be strong enough, and I'm going to be independent, so that I can work and take care of my children. Like, my mom does that. She's there for me when I need her, and she also has a career so that she's not just, like, sitting at home doing nothing. She has a purpose in life. I think people, you know, need a purpose in life. If you want to stay home with your children, and you feel that's the best thing for them, that's fine. But if you're the type of person that really needs something outside of that, then you need to have that opportunity.

This realization, in turn, fed Lynn's aspirations to engage in meaningful adult work that could make a contribution:

I know it's like more responsibility, but if I can feel like I'm doing something, I think my life has meaning. Like, I want to be a doctor. I want to be either an OB-GYN or a pediatric surgeon. And if I can, you know, take care of children and treat people, I think then my life has meaning because I'm doing something for someone else.

The practice of vocational discernment—figuring out what one's calling is and how to offer one's life—is a part of spirituality and religious life that sometimes fails to be recognized as such in a society that reduces the meaning of work to the acquisition of money or status. Elsewhere, Dori Grinenko Baker and I have written extensively on nurturing the vocational lives of adolescent girls.[4] What bears commenting on here, in relation to these girls' voices, is the power that mothers hold to bless the vocational strivings of their adolescent daughters when mothers engage in work that their daughters respect, admire, or find inspiring. As Jessica, a seventeen-year-old European American girl who is active in her United Methodist congregation, commented:

My mother is incredible. She is smart and beautiful and wonderful in dealing with people. Both my parents—their lives have been for unselfish reasons. . . . I love that I can be proud of them and all they've done. I think that's really important. . . . My mom works to put diversity in college curriculums, and she used to be a women's studies professor. . . . So my parents both do these really worthwhile, important things.

In this assessment of her parents' work, Jessica highlights not only the types of work her parents do, which she obviously admires, but also the motivations she perceives them to have. Commenting on her own vocational interests, Jessica said:

If you're asking what I want to do with my life, I want to be able to do things that I know are right . . . to look around and make sure I am doing something worthwhile. 'Cause that's part of what I mean when I say that's what I respect so much about my parents.

It might have surprised the mothers of these girls to know that they were held in such high regard by their daughters, because the same girls also spoke about tensions and struggles in their relationships with their mothers. Obviously, for these girls, admiration and conflict could coexist.

Connected Through Conflict

Ask girls about their relationships with their mothers, and many begin by narrating the most recent story of conflict. Nadine offered this example:

> My mom? Well, we're close. Except we fight all the time—on my way here, we had a big fight in the car—always about something stupid, like what I'm wearing, or how much my phone bill was this month. That's what it was about in the car on the way here. I get so mad. Yeah, we're really close. It's just that we fight.

Such comments might sound paradoxical to those for whom conflict holds only negative associations. What Nadine's remarks suggest, however, is that conflict is a means of connection in the relationship. Nadine stated that she did not particularly like her mother "getting into [her] business" by placing limits on the phone bill or determining acceptable clothing choices. What provoked Nadine's anger was her feeling that her mother was attempting to control her. At the same time, though, Nadine said:

> I know she does it because she cares. She cares how I present myself. She wants me to be okay. If she's arguing with me, then at least I know I matter to her.

Nadine's words illustrate one pattern that a number of these adolescent girls described in their relationships with their mothers: a "connected through conflict" form of mother-daughter relationship. Researchers have long noted that the period of early adolescence appears to be a time of accelerated conflict for mothers and daughters, and that girls experience more conflict with their mothers than boys do with either parent.[5] One of my ministry colleagues, David Berg, with whom I used to conduct grief-support groups for teens in drug treatment, regularly invited young people to create "body sculptures" of their tensive relationships with their parents. He asked them to pose their bodies, with another person representing a parent, to form a living sculpted image of the conflicted relationship. Adolescent girls frequently created sculptures in which they stood with hands and arms locked against the other person, both partners pushing against each other so that no movement resulted, but with a huge expenditure of effort and labor.

"What would happen to your sculpture if you let go and stopped fighting with your mom?" David would ask the girls.

Time after time, girls' faces registered the shock of recognition when, following his suggestion, they stopped fighting and let go of their parental stand-ins, only to find themselves altogether disengaged from the relationship. Struggle is one way to stay connected.

Girls describing this pattern of "connection through conflict" were focused on the tensive elements of their relationships with their mothers, and although not all of them put the kind of positive spin on the conflict that Nadine did, they each gave some indication that the conflict had helped them stay in relationship to their mothers during their adolescent years. As one young woman put it, "If we didn't have fighting, we wouldn't have nothing right now. So I guess that's worth something. It keeps us together, having things to fight about."

Certainly, increased conflict in relationships is one of the more difficult aspects of adolescence for parents (as well as for girls), especially if conflict stands in contrast to a relatively more harmonious parent-child relationship in childhood. Nearly every girl told about some kind of struggle or conflict in the recent history of her relationship with her mother. Girls who did not offer such stories in their interviews generally had less to say about their mothers overall.

Mother-daughter conflict in adolescence is certainly common, but is it inevitable? In 1904, G. Stanley Hall, a psychologist and professor, put his enduring stamp on the way twentieth-century Americans came to understand adolescence, characterizing it as a period of inevitable "storm and stress."[6] Only a few decades ago, in fact, it was common for scholars and researchers to characterize adolescence as a necessarily rebellious period full of stress and conflict. In their efforts to find developmental patterns that could help forge some way of understanding the often sharp transitions and strident behavior of youth, these earlier scholars framed adolescence in terms of hormonally driven identity-seeking behavior that inevitably involved a certain level of conflict and perhaps even rebellion against adults' norms and values.

Pipher, in her book *Reviving Ophelia,* also stands with this group of thinkers who view mother-daughter conflict as inevitable, given the cultural "rule" that girls must separate from their mothers in order to become adults. Pipher writes, "Growing up requires adolescent girls to reject the person with whom they are most closely identified. . . . Conflict between mothers and daughters is inevitable. To have a self, daughters must reject parts of their mothers. Always mothers and daughters must struggle with distance—too close and there is engulfment, too distant and there's abandonment."[7] Pipher's critique of the cultural situation in which girls must negotiate identity is helpful for pointing out the stress this situation creates for girls. But it also seems to buy into the idea that separation is necessary.

Because the stories we tell about our reality powerfully influence what we experience, our cultural narratives about mother-daughter conflict matter greatly. If the cultural story about adolescent girls and their mothers offers a picture in which the relationship is discolored by inevitable struggle, and in which conflict is interpreted as being principally about separation, then conflict undoubtedly will be experienced as a harbinger of the end of the relationship.

But contemporary research on adolescent girls has begun to offer a counternarrative to this story of necessary separation. Researchers now question the assumption that adolescence is primarily about dynamics of separation in relationships with parents and others. Instead, they understand the dynamics of transition in adolescence as having more to do with young people's renegotiation of their relationships with parents, other adults, and authority figures than with outright separation from those relationships. If the conflictual tension between an adolescent girl and her mother is not about separation, but about retooling the relationship into a different form as the girl clarifies her own sense of self, then the new story about this tension is a story of growth and change, not just of ending and loss. That is, the girl seeks to create a new kind of relationship with her mother, and she looks for new ways to relate to her mother that are more egalitarian and less hierarchical, in accordance with the girl's move toward young-adult status.

Particularly in the case of girls, the notion of adolescence as a time for renegotiating relationships offers a helpful understanding of adolescent emotional dynamics with respect to the developmental transition toward adulthood. Girls are not so much trying to move away from their mothers, through conflict, as they are struggling over new ways of relating to their mothers. These new ways have more to do with a daughter's establishing autonomy within the relationship than with her separating herself from the relationship. Conflict gives the adolescent girl a means of actively differentiating her emerging selfhood from the person of her mother.

Rona expressed well the sense of connection within conflict. She teared up when she described closeness in the midst of her conflicts with her mother:

> *How do you think your mother sees you as a person?*
>
> Oh, I think she sees me as very strong-willed. . . . Like, on the outside, I might seem, like, really hard, or whatever. But when you know me [starts to cry], like, you know what gets to me, things like that. She knows who I am . . . 'cause I fight with her a lot. And I'm free to say things like, "Oh, Mom, you annoy me when you do this"—things like that. She's so funny, because—a lot of times I say to her, "Mama, you're so annoying," and sometimes she'll say to me, "So what? You annoy me, too, sometimes." Yeah, she knows who I am.

Rona's family had come from Indonesia, and as she described her faith and her relationship with her mother, she also emphasized the role that cultural difference played in her conflicts with her parents:

> As I've grown older, I've gotten a little more free. I don't know how I've developed this, but, yeah, I started talking back a long, long time ago [*smiles*]. If my parents scream at me, I'll just yell something back. So sometimes I think it's disrespectful, but I like to blame it on, like, the American culture [*smiles again*], you know? The way I was raised by society, everyone talks back—everyone's on an equal level! And so they've just—well, I know my mom has become more of a friend. . . . In some ways, our relationship has gotten more open because I am more open.

Thus conflict may be one way for a girl to renegotiate what it means to be a daughter in new circumstances as she emerges into young adulthood. The tensions in the relationship actually help her forge new patterns. Whereas in childhood a girl might have simply acquiesced to her mother's authority, in adolescence her ability and desire to push back may be an important feature of her establishing a more egalitarian basis for the relationship. Obviously, this kind of action may involve considerable effort on the part of an adolescent girl, but the psychotherapist Janet Surry describes the attempt of a mother and an adolescent daughter to update their relationship as also requiring considerable effort on the mother's part:

> Clearly, both mothers and daughters often have difficulty getting "current" in their relationship. Mothers' memories hold the images of

their children as infants, and throughout life they continue to "see" (and therefore evoke) the child in their adolescent or adult children.[8]

Ana Mari Cauce and her colleagues contend that there may be significant variation between how white girls and black girls rework their relationships with their mothers in adolescence. According to these researchers, the need of African American mothers to help keep their daughters safe in the hostile environment of a racist society can sometimes work against these mothers' desire to promote the autonomy of their daughters, and what may look to outsiders like a harsher, more controlling style of parenting is instead a mode of promoting "autonomous relatedness" that also takes account of the historical and cultural experiences of African Americans in the United States.[9] The work of renegotiating the mother-daughter relationship is also taking place, but it may look different from the same work carried out in another racial or ethnic group.

Theological Discussion Partners

In my congregation, an event that parents and other adults look forward to at the conclusion of the confirmation class each year is the gathering in which young people share their "faith statements," public expressions of what they believe and how they understand their Christian faith. Last year, after all these statements had been read aloud and the meeting came to an end, I heard parents marveling to one another about the theological capacities of these youth.

"I had no idea she even thought about these things," said one surprised mother. "This is way beyond 'How did Noah get the animals to go onto the ark?' She's into complicated theology now!"

Girls come to YTI's summer academy with different backgrounds in theology from their experiences in Sunday school or other Christian education, in religion classes at parochial schools, or in church camps. They arrive with different levels of exposure to faith questions and theology. Some arrive already "into complicated theology"; others have had few opportunities to expand their ways of thinking about matters of faith beyond a more basic framework. These differences were reflected in the interviews, in which girls evidenced a variety of starting points for engaging in girl talk about faith and theology. What they had in common across these differences was their interest in discussion. The girls appreciated, valued, and sought out conversation partners for exploring theological issues. And for some of them, mothers were among the most esteemed conversation partners.

For instance, Jonelle named her mother as the primary person to whom she turned to discuss difficult matters of faith:

> As far as religious questions, I look to my mom because she has read a lot. She's got bookshelves of books, and she knows what she believes, but she's read the other side just to see, and I really respect that. She's so smart.

Similarly, other girls appreciated being able to talk with their mothers and share books addressing their faith questions. Pam, for example, had been surprised when the YTI group visited a congregation one Sunday and the pastor gave a theological rationale for gender inequality:

> I couldn't believe it, and I was upset about it, so I called my mom to talk it through with her. That's when she sent that book I told you about [*The Moral Teachings of Paul*, by Victor Paul Furnish, which Pam had mentioned earlier while describing resources that were helping her grow in her thinking]. It's a book that takes on a lot of issues that people pick out of Paul to try to justify things. I think that [book] had a really big influence on me. I told her what happened . . . with the Baptist minister saying women couldn't be ministers because it's in the Bible. She sent [the book] to me and highlighted some things.

For Pam, conversations and shared books were a valuable means by which her mother supported her religious life.

Religious Conflicts

Not all the girls who were interviewed reported such positive experiences with their mothers around faith talk. Some girls came from families in which the parents professed no faith, or in which anxiety about religiosity in the girls' own life experience colored their attempts to talk about questions of faith. For other girls, experiences with faith perspectives that were different from those of other family members were a source of tension when the girls tried to talk with their mothers about religion. Latoya, for example, described the conflict that arose with her mother as her own theological ideas began to differ significantly from those of her mother:

> I had some conversation with my mom where she was just completely convinced that I was no longer a Christian. We were talking about the Bible or something, and she was just, "I can't believe you said that!" We were talking about different religions, and I was, like, "Well, Mom, what if those other religions exist, and all of them in some way

are right? What if Christians have a piece of it that's generally right, and Buddhists have another piece that's generally right?" . . . My mom went crazy. She was, like, "I can't believe you are saying this! The Bible says that you have to such and such." She was quoting Romans, where Paul is, like, "Confess with your heart and believe. That is what you have to do, and if you don't do that, you are not saved. You are going straight to hell." . . . She just went nuts. . . . It is a constant argument with my mom, and she really was convinced that somehow she had failed, like I was going to go to hell or something.

Differences in faith perspectives and practices between mothers and their daughters can become a space for renegotiating the terms of the relationship. But because religion focuses on matters of ultimate concern, such as basic values and commitments in life, there can be much at stake when mothers and daughters encounter differences in their faith perspectives. Rona gave an example of this on the subject of religious doubts:

I remember in sixth grade, that's when I first had the thought that God—what if God didn't exist? And one day I came home to my mom, and I say, "Mom, what if God doesn't exist? What if we're doing all this for nothing?" And she got so mad! She's, like, "Rona!" I don't think she cried. She might have—she was on the verge of it. And she said, "Don't you ever question God." And I don't think I went any further with that, at that moment.

Rona said it felt as if to go "further with that" would have put her relationship with her mother at risk because of the apparent gravity her mother attached to Rona's questioning the existence of God. In this preadolescent time that she remembered, Rona did not push her point of view with her mother. In her later teen years, however, around the time of her interview, Rona had come to a different relationship with her mother, one in which it was all right to push back, to talk and disagree about such matters:

My mother, she's—I like her a lot because she tries to give me freedom to do stuff.

Do you feel close to her?

Very. Yeah. I talk to her about pretty much everything. She's, like, my best friend. She knows who I like at school, and things like that. But it's kind of funny—'cause whenever I talk to her about stuff like that, she never really responds, she just listens. Yeah, I'm very close to her. I tell her everything. And now we can have discussions about God and things like that, and she doesn't really mind. And I guess she likes that I'm examining my faith, and things like that.

It appears that in their relationship some conflict was useful in helping Rona reconfigure how she could relate to her mother from a more adult level.

In several interviews, girls depicted religious differences in their families, and with their mothers, as a significant source of conflict, which at times was not easily resolved. For example, a mother described by her daughter as a "strong feminist" objected to her daughter's participation in an evangelical Christian youth program. Said this daughter:

> I know that she's worried I'm going to turn into one of these conservative Christian women who believe that men are superior because God made them that way, or something. I'm not! I go to the youth group because I like the people, and because they have these little talks that help me think about where my beliefs in Jesus fit into everyday life. In our church, which my mom really likes, people are so busy doing things to change the world that hardly anyone talks about what it means to love and follow Jesus.

The mother, after weekly struggles over her daughter's desire to participate in this youth group, finally agreed to stop opposing her daughter's participation, in exchange for her daughter's commitment to spend some time every week talking with her mother about the group. Eventually the mother was reassured about the content of this group's programming, and it ceased to be a source of conflict.

Research on conflict in adolescents' relationships with their parents points to early adolescence as the time of most intense conflict, which then tapers off toward the later teen years. One factor in this tapering effect may be related to the gradual "solidifying" of some of the boundaries of difference between mother and daughter that come to constitute what Gilligan and Brown term the "self-in-relationship."[10] That is, girls in later adolescence may experience less of a need to press the points of distinction between themselves and their mothers, because some of the negotiations toward new ways of relating have borne fruit.

Adolescent Empathy

Another factor in the tapering off of conflict is the ability of teens later in their high school years to have a larger perspective on parental actions and motivations than is possible in the earlier years of adolescence. That is, girls begin to recognize their mothers as people with their own interior lives and are more willing and able to grant that their mothers think and do things that are independent of their daughters' lives and concerns. In later adolescence, many of the girls I interviewed demonstrated an ability to reconsider the judgments of their mothers that they had made in earlier years, and they looked with new understanding at the choices their mothers had made and the actions they had taken. For example, Sarah, describing her feelings toward her mother, who "always [had] to work late," said that earlier in her teen years she and her mother had not always been able to get along very well:

> I was resentful of her, probably unfairly, because we never had the normal family life. . . . I don't feel resentful toward her anymore, because I know that it's not her fault. I mean, she didn't have any other choice. And I guess when I was littler, I didn't understand the seriousness of it. But now [I see that] just to keep a roof over our heads, food, clothes, all that stuff, she *had* to do that. It wasn't, like, a choice she made, so I don't feel like that toward her anymore.

Here, Sarah was talking about feeling greater compassion for her divorced mother, a single parent, and about recently having become more sympathetic to her mother's situation and able to see her mother as a person who had faced and dealt with serious dilemmas. Before, she had been locked into conflict with her mother, resentful over choices made by her mother that had affected Sarah's life. Now, in later adolescence, Sarah could cut her mother some slack, whereas before she had thought about her mother's long work hours, and her parents' decision to end their marriage, mainly in terms of the negative impacts on her own life. Now those earlier judgments were being reassessed, and a certain rapprochement had taken place.

Like Sarah, other girls in later adolescence also become willing to grant that, at least sometimes, their mothers' choices may have been the best ones in the circumstances. The work by Gilligan and Rogers on mother-daughter relationships in adolescence suggests that this capacity for deeper empathy and understanding reflects cognitive and emotional growth that "make possible a different kind of relationship between mother and daughter, in part because the daughter is better able to feel and see into her mother's life."[11]

Many of the girls I interviewed demonstrated this reflective capacity, which allowed them to have a measure of understanding for their parents, even in situations of conflict. Raquel, for example, had this to say about the conflict in her relationship with her mother:

> As far as my mother goes, she's sort of like a friend to me. But, you know, every once in a while she does little things that really get to me, pluck my nerves and drive me crazy. But still, you know, even when I get angry with her, I realize that I love her. She's just doing this to, obviously, help me somehow in the long run. Or . . . usually she's right, and I just didn't want to see it her way. But we have a close relationship. We still do things together. I try to spend time with her, like, as much as I can, along with my friends. Because, you know, sometimes when your friend's not there, your mother's still gonna be there for you.

It may be that mother-daughter conflict, just as it can play a beneficial role in an adolescent daughter's identity development, can also facilitate a girl's religious life. The ability to move from judgment and critique to compassionate understanding represents a significant spiritual transformation in a girl's life. And it happens, at least in part, because of her mother's simple willingness to stay connected with her daughter through conflict.

Mothers thus participate in the religious lives of their daughters, even without any particular intention to do so, as their differing theological perspectives, or the absence of parental faith, become occasions for girls to explore these contrasts with their own beliefs and practices. Girls like Latoya are able to make use of conflict to sharpen their own thinking and refine what really matters to them in how they practice their faith. Girls like Sarah struggle with their mothers through early adolescence but move toward a more generous rapprochement in their later teen years, when expanded cognitive and affective capacities make the spiritual quality of empathy deeper in this relationship.

Conflict never feels good, but it can be beneficial, so an important aspect of supporting a daughter's religious life may be her mother's ability to remain present and active in the conflict instead of retreating to a comfort zone in separation from her daughter. This is not a call for confrontational mothering; rather, it is a call for mothers to recognize that, because conflict can be so painful, the natural tendency may be to retreat from it, even though daughters need their mothers to stay engaged with them through conflict. Terri Apter's studies of mother-daughter relationships in the United States and Great Britain, for example, show that girls hope for relationships with their mothers that are challenging and lively; girls want to know that their mothers' commitment to them overrides disagreements and conflicting positions in a debate.[12] What Apter's work also shows, however—a finding echoed in the work of Debold, Brown, Weseen, and Brookins[13]—is that far too often mothers retreat from conflicts, disagreements, and hard discussions with their daughters, depriving girls of the opportunity to experience maternal commitment that goes beyond simple agreement and shared perspectives. Mothers who retreat in this way, instead of framing the meaning of conflict in terms of a reconfigured mother-daughter relationship, are operating from the cultural narrative that conflict with daughters has to do with a necessary separation.

As several of these interviews show, it is significant that faith-based differences, although they can become a source of tension and conflict in mother-daughter relationships, can also become the basis of important forms of connection as daughters attempt to work out their beliefs and practices. Sometimes such moves by a daughter will require her mother to shift from a directing role in her daughter's religious life to a more advisory role, one in which the mother simply listens or attempts to talk with her daughter about the implications or consequences of religious ideas and actions.

When Mom Doesn't Believe

Sometimes mothers are indifferent to the religion and spirituality that matter so greatly in the lives of their daughters. This situation was somewhat rare among the group of girls participating in my interview research project, but a few girls spoke of their religious lives as completely outside any shared sphere of relationship with their mothers. As one girl put it:

> My mom totally does not get this Christianity thing. She would never go to any church. She says what matters is how you live, not where you spend Sunday mornings. Well, okay, but I keep trying to tell her that where I spend Sunday mornings helps me figure out how I live.

In the particular group of girls who were my research partners, the situation of an indifferent or nonbelieving mother did not appear to pose any special crisis or difficulty for those girls for whom it was a reality. I have known girls, however, particularly among evangelical church communities, for whom a mother's lack of religious involvement was a source of anxiety because of the meanings the girls attributed to their mothers' lack of faith. One of these girls, whose mother had been diagnosed with terminal breast cancer, expressed her devastation over her understanding that she would not be reunited with her mother in heaven because her mother was not a Christian believer. An astute pastoral counselor was able to work with the girl and her mother in terms of their anticipatory grief. The counselor further helped the daughter expand her theological perspectives to imagine the possibility that the same God who loved and had saved her, the daughter, would not want her mother to be eternally separated from her. And the mother was able to articulate a broad, general belief in God, as the spirit of compassion and love at work in the world, so that she could meet her daughter partway.

Sometimes, however, a genuine impasse occurs. A mother lacks belief, and a daughter feels that everything important depends on belief. Or a mother's religious understanding differs so significantly from that of her daughter that their perspectives appear completely incompatible, and the two of them are placed at loggerheads with each another. It would be false to suggest that all situations of difference between mothers and daughters can be resolved by compromise or easily negotiated into agreement. Perhaps at such times the best that can be hoped for is that the differences can be negotiated into a truce, a state where mother and daughter can each live with the differences in the other's beliefs, even though these differences remain important to them, and even though the two of them continue to disagree. In all kinds of relationships, people effect arrangements whereby they agree to disagree yet stay connected. The important issue for mothers and daughters in this situation is the tone of the disagreement: if nonbelieving or differently believing mothers show outright hostility toward their daughters' religiosity, that undermines and damages the relationship.

There was a period during my high school years when I participated in a nondenominational Christian group in addition to being a member of the youth ministry at the Presbyterian Church to which I belonged. My mother did not particularly endorse the theological viewpoints of this other group, but she also seemed to recognize that opposition from her would probably backfire and encourage me to make the group more important than it actually was to me. Years later, she told me she had figured that as long as this group wasn't dangerous to me, she trusted that I would, as she said, "have the sense eventually to grow out of it." She was right, in the sense that my theology soon moved beyond the boundaries set by the group's highly individualistic and personalistic understanding of Christian faith. But I am also aware that my involvement with that group was part of my own religious identity differentiation and development, and that it contributed something important to my emerging sense of selfhood that remains with me today. And I am grateful that my mother had the wisdom not to allow our difference to become a major division between us. We had enough other struggles to worry about, without also arguing over religion!

Reflections

Apter, writing nearly twenty years ago about mothers and their adolescent daughters, attempted to put to rest the notion that girls want to be left alone by their mothers:

> The adolescent does not develop her identity and individuality by moving outside her family. She is not triggered by some magic unconscious dynamic whereby she rejects her family in favour of her peers or of a larger society. . . . She continues to develop in relation to her parents. Her mother continues to have more influence over her than either her father or her friends.[14]

This continuing influence by mothers, attested to by psychologists, researchers, educators, and physicians, occurs in the midst of the relationship's transformation.

In this chapter, I have described listening to girls who told me about how their religious perspectives had participated in reshaping their relationships with their mothers. These girls also described various ways in which their mothers had influenced their religious lives, and they marked points of similarity and difference between themselves and their mothers in terms of how they saw faith and gender identity. Their mothers clearly played a continuing and significant role in the religious lives of these daughters. At the same time, the girls indicated that, although they were actively constructing their beliefs, values, and faith practices out of what their families had modeled for them, they were also, as adolescents, able to make meaning and build practices out of what they had found to resist and critique in their families. As one who cares about girls, and as a mother with a daughter, I find that a hopeful situation.

As I write this, my daughter, Sarah, who is now nine, is rapidly approaching early adolescence. This past winter, she played indoor soccer. In one game, in which she played with particular strength and energy, Sarah happened to be involved in three incidents in which a ball that she had kicked accidentally hit and injured another player (in one case, the ball also knocked the hat off the referee). Each time, Sarah stopped play and ran over to assist the hurt player. When play resumed, Sarah stood with tears as well as sweat streaking down her face. Her coach assured

Sarah that the other players were all right (so did the referee and the girls themselves), and that these kinds of small injuries were to be expected in the game. Sarah continued to play, but a bit less vigorously. When I was finally able to talk with her, at halftime, she exclaimed that she was not sure she wanted to play anymore.

"It's too hard for me when I hurt people! I feel too upset for them."

I started encouraging her to recognize this as an acceptable level of hurt, but she interrupted me.

"Mama, I learned from you about standing up for people who are down, and that we always want to try not to be the cause of hurting someone. So even though I know this is just a game, it's inside of me that it's not good to hurt anyone. Do you now want me to believe something different?"

This was, for me, a moment of recognition that Sarah, at nine, holds some very good values and has the confidence to say what she believes. And, as a preadolescent girl, she does not yet have all the cognitive, emotional, and moral features that will allow her, in a few more years, to discern more particularly between one situation and another, to make informed judgments about her actions. There is something dear about the black-and-white logic of preadolescent thinking that I know will be lost under the impact of new, adolescent abilities to wrestle with ambiguity and dwell in the gray areas of moral issues. In that moment, I also recognized that I remain important in Sarah's religious life and moral development. I have a role in fostering her religious beliefs and practices.

As we rapidly go together into her adolescent years, I anticipate many more times when she will feed back to me what I have said or taught, values I've affirmed as well as transgressed, as we sort anew through our relationship, shifting the balance of power from that of parent and young child to that of parent and emerging young adult. That day on the soccer field, Sarah asked me what I now wanted for her. I want her to be physically and emotionally strong. I hope that she will have a vibrant faith that moves her out into the world with the same sense of care and justice that she brings to her empathy for downed soccer players. And I hope and trust that we will continue to live our lives deeply connected to each other, however differently our connection may be configured.

5

GIRL TALK ON FATHERS

JILL, A TALL THIN GIRL with a single long braid of hair trailing down her back, smiled when asked about her relationship with her father. After a brief pause, she said:

> It's funny that you should ask. I just got off the phone with him a few minutes ago. We've been talking a lot since I got here [YTI]—in fact, maybe more than before. I think he just figured out that I'm not going to be at home forever, so he'd better make the most of it now! I think our relationship is really changing. *He's* really changing. He's more of a—well, you know, more of a *dad* than he used to be.

Jill went on to describe growing up in a Midwestern suburban neighborhood where many mothers were at home with their children, and fathers went off to work in the city each day,

> and that's how it was in our family, too. I didn't really see my dad that much growing up. Then he got sick and had to quit work for a while. That started the changes two years ago. He took us to school in the mornings. He was the one at home when we got home. Sort of like *Mr. Mom!* [*Laughter.*] He was the one who drove me to confirmation class, and so we'd argue a lot about different ideas of God and the church. My dad is very bright, very thoughtful. He helped me with the theological problem of why God would let someone like him get so sick—why there are wars and poverty if God is good. That's the kind of thing I like to talk to him about. We've gotten a lot closer over the last couple of years.

Jill paused in her reflections, looked somber for a moment, then concluded:

> Imagine if I had been born in a different time, before it was okay for fathers to stay at home. I might *never* have gotten to know him!

Inviting girls to reflect on their relationships with their fathers is like administering a group Rorschach test whose results depict the changing character of fatherhood in contemporary U.S. society. That is, in the various ways in which girls described their current relationships and their histories with their fathers, including their yearnings and disappointments, they offered images not only of their personal experiences in these relationships but also of the kinds of cultural fantasies of fatherhood that had shaped their imaginations. Their descriptions of their dads displayed outlines of the seismic transformations that fathers and fatherhood have undergone in this country over the past half-century.

Many of these girls, born in the early 1980s or later, expressed the expectation that their fathers would be much more involved in their daughters' everyday lives than my peers or I ever would have expected our fathers to be. I loved my father and looked forward to the times we spent together, but in many of my childhood memories he is leaving for work or arriving home from work, smelling of sawdust and fresh lacquer spray from his cabinet shop. I did not expect to have large amounts of time with him that were focused on my interests and activities, nor did I expect my father to have much to do with my day-to-day maintenance. He was not the parent who made my lunch or attended school conferences. The novelist Margaret Atwood's depiction of fathers rang true for me and undoubtedly for many others in my age cohort: "All fathers are invisible in daytime; daytime is ruled by mothers, and fathers come out at night."[1]

Today that level of paternal "daytime invisibility" has simply ceased to be the case for many girls as norms for men and their roles in family life undergo transformation. My daughter, for example, is far more likely to come home from school to her dad as the snack preparer and homework helper than she is to find me there in those roles. Similarly, for the girls who were my interview partners, dads rated high in terms of their importance and involvement in their daughters' everyday lives, regardless of whether they were physically present in their daughters' homes on a daily basis. Against the stereotype that girls can be close to their fathers only when their fathers are living at home with them, girls whose fathers did not share a home with them still reported having close relationships with fathers who took time to learn about and attend their musical and athletic performances, or who talked to them regularly about their lives.

On the whole, the girls I interviewed had experienced their fathers in early childhood as more involved in their day-to-day care, education, and emotional lives than the fathers of yesteryear ever were. Therefore, these girls expected and experienced a different kind of involvement with their fathers during adolescence, too. And even when fathers were unavailable, not physically or emotionally an element in their daughters' lives—because they were absent or in some other way disconnected—their daughters still saw contemporary fathers' greater degree of involvement as a social standard by which to assess and judge their own family situations and their own fathers.

In one or two instances when a girl claimed that her father was not at all important to her, the emotional tenor of her words and what she said about other people's fathers belied her claims of indifference. Her father—missing in action, rarely seen or heard from—was *negatively* important in terms of what was *not* happening in his relationship with his daughter. It seems that fathers occupied an important place in the lives of most of these adolescent girls, whether that place was one of bright, glowing affection, strongly negative emotions, or deep ambivalence. Whatever a father's place, he mattered, and he exerted an important influence on the life of his adolescent daughter.

Learning from Girl Talk on Fathers

Listening to girl talk on fathers surfaced several interesting discoveries about the relationships between adolescent girls and their dads. It might be surprising for some fathers to know, for example, that these girls cared about their fathers' opinions, and especially about how their fathers regarded their daughters. They expressed interest in their fathers as conversation partners. They cared about their fathers' religious understandings and practices, and many girls articulated a longing for their fathers to share in their daughters' religious interests. They also expressed interest in their fathers as people, not just as embodiments of the father's role in their own lives. They felt pride in the kinds of work done by their fathers and had a sense that their dads were making a contribution to the lives of others.

I also learned a lot from these girls about how much power their fathers had in their daughters' lives. Some of this power was explicitly negative and harmful. For instance, girls talked about the power their fathers had to wound them by unintended slights with temporary effects, such as when a father made a joke that inadvertently pushed a daughter's buttons on a matter where she felt vulnerable. They also spoke of their fathers being in a position to hurt them much more deeply with verbal abuse, and a few girls spoke of their fathers' abuse of power through physical violence in their homes.

But, along with such stories of fathers' harmful use of power in father-daughter relationships, many girls attributed to their fathers an interesting positive power: the power to bless them. That is, these girls expressed a strong desire for their fathers to affirm them. They longed for their fathers to recognize and take pleasure in their accomplishments. They wanted their emerging young-adult selves to be noticed, honored, and valued.

The power to bless is a spiritual power with deep resonance in the Christian tradition's biblical stories of fathers blessing their children. In the patriarchal world of the Hebrew scriptures, of course, most of these stories are about fathers blessing their sons (such as the story from Genesis 27, in which a crafty younger son, Jacob, manages to "steal" the paternal blessing from his older brother, Esau). Daughters, if they were in these stories at all, stood in the background, watching others receive the blessings.

Nowadays, we who are parents seek to bless both our sons and our daughters. And in this day and age, we recognize that the spiritual power of blessing belongs not only to fathers but also to mothers, teachers, coaches, and many others involved in the lives of adolescent girls. In my interviews with this group of girls, however, their longing to be blessed by their fathers was quite pronounced. Girls who had received their fathers' blessing celebrated this aloud; girls who lacked the blessing of their fathers spoke in various ways, mostly indirect, of their desire for it and their often frustrated efforts to secure it.

What do these findings suggest for fatherly support of the spiritual lives of girls? Fathers are well situated to contribute to the religious lives of their daughters. They do so as companions, conversation partners, and role models. In some instances, they may inadvertently have a negative influence, for it seems that girls must develop spiritual resources to help them cope with pain and difficulty in their relationships with their fathers. And fathers clearly contribute to the spiritual lives of girls through their power to bless them.

What's the Difference?

Are the contributions made by fathers to the spiritual lives of adolescent girls really so different from those of mothers? By discussing these contributions separately, I may seem to be saying so: "Fathers do x, y, and z, and mothers do a, b, and c." And, indeed, much research literature and popular writing on father-daughter relationships from the past five decades hones in on the precise question of a father's distinctive contribution to his daughter's development.[2] But, as the previous chapter shows, it is not my intent to assert that only fathers engage in deep theological conversations with girls or have the power to bless them. I am not saying that fathers, through their engagement with meaningful work, are more significant role models for their daughters than mothers are. I am not so much trying to compare mothers and fathers as to depict how the girls in these interviews talked about each of these parental relationships, and to see what can be learned from girl talk on fathers.

Cultural Fantasies of Fatherhood

Just as these girls reflected certain cultural idealizations in their depictions of their mothers, so also, when they talked about their dads, did they reflect the impact of cultural fantasies about fathers, or what Ralph LaRossa, in his sociopolitical history of fatherhood, calls "fatherhood as the product of people's collective imagination."[3] LaRossa's point is that fatherhood involves both a social role and a sociohistorical institution. It consists of certain norms that men are expected to follow when they become fathers. What any particular father does in his role as a dad— who he is as a father—is action taken in a larger culture of fatherhood, which involves cultural values as well as power relations between groups of people (particularly between men and women); fathering is informed by social attitudes toward fathers, by a society's collective knowledge of what fathers in the past have done, and by "the routine activities of men when they are trying to be 'fatherly.' "[4]

The power of such cultural fantasies to produce particular kinds of relationships between fathers and daughter showed up in girls' discussions of what constitutes a good father. The cultural scripts to which the girls alluded included complex images of fathers as protectors of their daughters, as gatekeepers of romantic access to them, and as conduits to the worlds of higher education and work. The girls' descriptions of what constitutes a good father were variations on a theme expressed by Kit:

> [He] lets me know that I am physically attractive, from a male point of view, and then acts like a protector from other males—like, guys my age—who also think I'm attractive but might want the wrong thing.

And, as Joanne said, a good dad

> takes you out into the world and shows you around. My dad takes me to his work, helps me know what it's like to be an adult.

Not all girls were this explicit in expressing their cultural fantasies of fathers, either as romantic gatekeepers or as conduits to the adult world beyond the domestic sphere. But when girls did use these figures of speech, their voices joined similar ones in the psychological literature on father-daughter relationships, voices that, beginning with Freud, have named fathers as the psychological means by which girls experience the separation from their mothers deemed necessary for achieving adulthood. Much contemporary research on fathers and fatherhood reflects the view that father-daughter relationships have the important function of assisting adolescent daughters in separating from their (negatively construed) symbiotic relationships with their mothers. Because separation from the mother has been the reigning understanding of what is necessary for maturity, psychologists who accept this viewpoint have understood the function of a girl's relationship with her father in terms of effecting this separation.

Such understandings rest on stereotypical gender roles—men as providers and protectors whose lives "naturally" open out into the public sphere of the wider world (which they offer, in partial ways, to their daughters), and women as hearth tenders, nurturers, and caregivers whose focus is interior, toward relationships and the family. Thus these perspectives depend on the assumption that women's maturation into adulthood necessarily depends on the separation from their mothers that is brought about by their fathers. This assumption has been questioned by women's psychologies. Nevertheless, quite a few of the girls in this interview group obviously had internalized this cultural understanding of fatherhood, and it had shaped their experiences of their particular fathers, primarily in terms of their fathers' roles as protectors and as bridges to the wider public world outside the home.

The social historian Rachel Devlin details what she calls the "eroticisation of the father-daughter relationship" in post–World War II America, finding in such artifacts of popular culture as theater, women's magazines, and literature depictions of fathers as key figures in their daughters' adolescent sexual development.[5] From this psychologized perspective, a girl who does not have a good relationship with her father is destined to have unhappy relationships with men, and her achievements in the world will also be truncated.

I do not wish to overstate the strength of this cultural fantasy of fatherhood in girls' conversations about their fathers. Rather, I simply note its presence in many of the interviews, and the way it functions as a societal answer to the question "What is the unique role of a father in the life of his adolescent daughter?" And, like cultural fantasies of mothers, such images and imaginary standards do have a role in shaping how girls experience and evaluate their actual fathers.

Competing Scripts on Fathers

Some years ago, when I was involved in clinical work with chemically dependent teens, my colleagues and I noticed that father loss seemed to be an especially powerful grief experience in the lives of the adolescent girls with whom we worked. These girls often displayed more emotional volatility in their efforts to address the loss of their fathers than did their peers with other types of losses. They seemed to get stuck more frequently, and to have more trouble working through their pain, anger, anxiety, and sadness.

Over time, we surmised that one factor informing these girls' difficulties had to do with societal expectations about the relative importance and meaning of the father-daughter relationship. Such expectations are found in two competing "scripts" that girls receive.

One of these I will call the "unimportant father" script. According to this perspective, the relationship that matters most for teenage girls is the one they have with their mothers; thus the loss of her father is deemed relatively less significant for a girl. In other words, it should be no big deal to her when she experiences a loss of relationship with her father, because—ostensibly, at least—he is not that important anyway. According to the "unimportant father" script, fathers make little if any distinctive contributions to the lives of their daughters.

The other script, which I will call the "all-important father" script, attributes near-ultimate significance to a father's presence and involvement with his daughter. In this script, fathers are the heroes of their families, and especially of their daughters, bequeathing to them the ability to have strong, positive relationships with other males and to succeed in the worlds of education and work. According to the "all-important father" script, the loss of her father practically dooms a girl to a legacy of dysfunctional relationships with men and difficulties achieving satisfaction or success in the adult world of work.

But girls who experience this kind of loss are not the only ones encountering these scripts on father-daughter relationships. What my listening to girl talk on fathers tells me is that these competing cultural fantasies about fathers probably have a strong impact on the way girls experience their relationships with their fathers. It is not always easy for a girl to describe her father or her relationship with him, and when she does so, she understandably make use of the images and ideas that are available to her in the wider cultural context in which she lives. Thus the girls who were my partners in these interviews painted multilayered, sometimes contradictory portraits of their fathers and their relationships with them.

A Time for Dads to Grow Up

How did girls view their relationships with their fathers from the vantage point of late adolescence? Most of the girls with whom I spoke about their relationships with their dads recognized their relationships as being in transition, a situation they tended to attribute to their own growth and development as young women on the brink of adulthood. A few girls, however, recognized the transitional status of their relationships as occasioned by changes in their fathers as well as in themselves. For example, Leslie, a suburban European American girl who was very involved in the life and leadership of her church, began her description of her relationship with her father by remarking, "We are in transition right now." She then spoke about how different the two of them were from one each other, naming her involvement in her church as an example of their differences that she sometimes found difficult. Her father, she said, was not very involved in church himself, although he supported her involvement. Sometimes, however, he had a hard time expressing that support in ways she could appreciate:

> He teases a lot, and I had to learn to deal with that. That's his way of saying, "I'm proud of you for what you're doing." Even though that's hard to understand.
>
> *It hasn't always been something you've understood as positive?*
>
> No, no. There was a time when I used to get so mad at him for teasing me. Now I just kinda say, that's the way he is, you know, it's part of him.
>
> *Is it a factor that his expression of faith is different than yours?*
>
> I think it's a lot of it. I don't think he would really understand how important the church is to me. I don't think anyone who's not involved in church like I am could ever understand. You have to experience it to know what it's really like, and to know the strength that I get from that, and I think that's a lot of it. He hasn't had that experience. He doesn't know how important it is.

Leslie went on to say how difficult it was for her that her father could not really understand her interest in wanting to become a minister, even though she felt she could count on his support.

Despite these differences, as Leslie described her present relationship with her father, she emphasized an increase in the length, frequency, and depth of their conversations as partly responsible for the transition to a closer relationship. She described a situation in which her mother and her brother had gone on a trip, leaving her father as the only family member who was there to receive her calls home:

> A couple of nights ago when I called Dad, we talked for about twenty-five minutes. It was really neat to talk, just to talk to him.
>
> *It sounds like that's new.*
>
> Yeah. It is, kinda. It's never been—when I would call home, and Mom and my brother were still home, I would talk to Dad for a couple of minutes and then talk to Mom for about ten minutes, then talk to my brother for a couple of minutes, and then hang up. It was neat to just talk to him for a long time.
>
> *How would you describe your relationship with your dad right now?*
>
> It's getting better. I mean, I just remember there were times when it was really hard to talk to him about anything. But talking about what I was going to do this summer—because I had several options, and I had a hard time deciding which one to do—looking at college, a lot of major decisions have come up that will impact the rest of my life. We started talking more and more, and we've grown closer. I think I'm growing up, and *he's* growing up, and it's easier [for him] to do that [talk], you know. It's hard [for a father] to have real deep discussions about high intellectual things with a six-year-old, and I think that's a big part of it.

Like Jill, whom we met at the beginning of this chapter, Leslie emphasized the new depths of her talk with her father as significant to her. She commented on her own processes of development as a contributing factor ("I'm growing up . . . it's hard to have . . . deep discussions . . . with a six-year-old"), and she spoke as well of her father's part in their discussions, in a way that suggested her awareness of his own interiority as a person ("*he's* growing up"). It seemed as if Leslie's father was becoming a person to her—someone with his own perspectives and experiences, to whom she could relate—and not just a role. This process parallels what I described in the previous chapter as girls' increasing capacity to recognize the interior lives and personhood of their mothers and thus to have new empathy with them.

Leslie described an important turning point in her relationship with her dad that occurred when a crisis presented her father with the opportunity to express his unequivocal support and care for her:

> A year ago this past spring, I was playing in an orchestra concert and wrecked the car right out in front of our house, and, um, I had my cello in the back seat. And I glanced behind and looked up and had gone off the road, into a tree. And I wasn't hurt—the car had a lot of damage to it—but I was scared stiff. I was just sitting there, frozen, and Dad had seen what happened and ran up and unlocked the door and pulled me out of the car and hugged me. And it's, like, looking back, then I knew he really cared about me. To this day, he still hasn't asked me what happened or how it happened. It's just, "Are you okay?" And that really— at that point, I really knew how much he loved me. But that was really, really powerful. I can also—when I was a sophomore, I applied for a scholarship to spend my junior year in Germany, and I was a finalist but didn't get the scholarship. I was really, really upset about that. And I remember him being real supportive about that and saying, "I'm proud of you." I think as I've gotten older, he's said that more and more.

Leslie's father blessed her in moments when she felt vulnerable and perhaps most unworthy of being blessed. Her awareness of her father's more frequent expressions of pride in her indicates the truth of her earlier statement: that as she matures, her father is also changing in relation to her. He is, in effect, also growing up, changing what he does in response to his daughter's needs for more explicit affirmation and blessing by offering "more and more" of both.

One of the gifts our children give to us is our identity as parents. It is their existence with us, and nothing else, that constitutes us as mothers and fathers. The season of adolescence underscores the fluidity of parental identity: who we are as mothers and fathers, how we parent, must undergo shifts and transformations in order to adjust to the shifts and transformations in our children. Amidst all the physical, emotional, and spiritual transformations teens are going through, it is tempting to believe that they are the ones who are changing while parents stay the same. What girls like Leslie describe, though, is their own awareness, appreciation, and profound respect for fathers who are willing to change with them.

Taking Dads off Their Pedestals

Unlike Leslie, who began with the observation that she and her father were really different, Alyssa opened her comments about her changing relationship with her dad by noting a characteristic they had in common—namely, a hot temper:

> I think that my relationship with my father has changed recently. He—we're a lot alike. We've always been really close, my dad and I—and, I mean, my mom and I, too—but my dad and I have [been especially close]. Um, but I think lately, because he's gotten in touch with—I don't know, my impending departure from the nest, and everything, I don't know—it's started to get to him, or something. But it's, like, sometimes I feel like he's pushing me away just because he doesn't want to be h—I don't know, hurt, or something. I don't have any idea. But it's, like, he just, um, he kind of picks fights with me. I mean, not pick fights, but—the morning before I left to come here, I, like, didn't shut the garage door, or something. And he's, like, "Why didn't you shut the garage door?" And of course I got mad because he was getting mad at me over something stupid. And, I don't know—I just feel like lately I've been stepping away from this relationship and going, "Okay, what do we need to fix here? There's something wrong." We always had a good relationship. And as I've gotten older, it's kind of changed in that, um—just naturally, I see more of his shortcomings, and everything. And that kind of worship [of my dad] is gone, in a way.

Two elements stand out in Alyssa's comments.

First, she used sophisticated skills of relational analysis in an effort to understand her father. His actions seemed strange, even foreign to her childhood ways of knowing her dad, by which he apparently had seemed more "perfect," less human than he appeared from her adolescent vantage point. But she did not merely engage in critiquing her father's now visible flaws. Instead, Alyssa tried to think about what was going on from her father's point of view, and she concluded that he picked fights with her as a way of pushing her away so it would not hurt so much when she left home. In her reflections, she used her ability to construct his (possible) internal experience to make sense of an event occurring between them. In the process, she constructed a portrait of her father as a human being struggling with issues of closeness and separation in relation to his daughter, in some very nonheroic but wonderfully human ways.

Second, Alyssa recognized that some of the change in their relationship arose from her adolescent ability to take her father off the pedestal he had occupied for her in childhood ("I see more of his shortcomings . . . that kind of worship is gone"). This acknowledgment that she could see her father's shortcomings did not appear to get in the way of her relationship with him. In fact, in her descriptions she tended to intersperse comments about these "shortcomings" with other remarks about how he was a "special person," almost as if she saw her father as special precisely because she knew he was not perfect:

And so, if you were going to describe him as a person now, from your perspective today, how would you do that?

Um . . . he's a really special person. I mean, he didn't have a good family situation growing up, but my dad's, like, just a real people person. You know, he gets along with people really well. And . . . he's a really good teacher. And he has some shortcomings to deal with, just the family situation being too [chaotic], and I think my dad's more controlling. Not, like, "You are going to do this," but more in a subtle—I don't want to say more manipulative, because that has bad connotations— but just in a more subtle kind of way, you know. But, you know, he's really a very special person. I still love him a whole lot, even though I refused to talk to him for the past week because he made me mad. [Laughter.] He came—they came, my family came down on Saturday, and they were, like, two and a half hours late because my dad found something that he needed to do. And it just really, really made me mad, so I haven't called them this week. Not that I'm manipulative or subtle or anything about it! [Laughter.] You know, it's just—those are the ways that I'm like him.

Alyssa spoke with a sense of humor about being like her father, of understanding what she called his "shortcomings" because she shared them. She commented, here and elsewhere, about how good her father was in his job, speaking with pride about his many responsibilities and his "people skills." She painted an interesting picture of the maturing closeness between them, in which her awareness of her father's flaws in no way cancelled out her delight in the type of work he did and the way he went about it. Alyssa and Leslie both offered a window onto how a father and a daughter can be close even while they move through somewhat disorienting transitions, and even conflict, during the girl's adolescence.

Absent Dads

Not all the girls with whom I spoke had fathers living in their households. Sometimes this situation was temporary, as in Jan's family, where issues of work and immigration had required her father to live away from the family for a few years:

I saw my mom more often than I saw my dad. Like, I have very few childhood memories of my dad, 'cause he used to, I guess—'cause he worked so much. And sometimes he went to—like, he had business

trips for a year before we moved to America. He was here for about
a year or two.

But reasons other than work kept some other girls' fathers away, and
these absences often occasioned conflicted feelings toward these fathers, or
distance in relationships with them. Mikela, for example, described a family
situation that had involved her parents' divorce when she was small:

> My mother is a single parent. I know my father. I remember living
> with him. But he wasn't there when I needed him, so . . . like, the first
> few years, I remember—not really anything. I just remember him
> being there, and going places with him, and stuff. Then I remember,
> when they started to split up, my mother would mostly sleep with me.
> I just remember him being a father figure until he left. But as far as
> people say[ing], "You need your father," I don't think I really do.
> Because everything—my mother, she's fulfilled all my needs, my paren-
> tal needs, and stuff. It would be nice to have a father. I mean, I have
> one, and I go see him, and he comes to see me every so often, but it's
> not close. I mean, he wants—he expects me to, like, treat him, I guess,
> affectionately. But I can't. I can't fake affection.

> *Is he important in your life in any way?*

> Not really. I don't know. I could do without him. I mean, I have, I
> guess, when I was small and we lived in the city. You know—I mean,
> I don't remember us being poor, like we see some of the people. I
> mean, I wasn't deprived of anything. It just would have helped my
> mother.

Mikela's comments about her father's absence underscored the economic
impact that a father's absence has on a family. And although Mikela said
clearly that her mother's parenting was sufficient, she also alluded to
some emotional stress at not having had an involved father:

> When we talk on the phone, after he finishes he says, "I love you."
> Sometimes I say it back, but sometimes I don't feel like saying it. I do
> love him because he's my father, but it's hard to say it. I think he just
> wants the power to control me.

Mikela also recalled times of seeing peers who had close relationships
with their dads and wishing she could have that kind of relationship herself. "But when I get married, it will be different," she remarked, her way
of saying she intended for her future children to have their father present
and available in their lives.

About a quarter of the girls in my interview group came from families in which the parents' divorce meant that the fathers did not reside with their children. A few of these girls described having had strong connections with their dads, even across different household configurations. But for others, the father's physical absence translated into loss of the father-daughter relationship. On the one hand, these girls' ability to find what they needed from other adults, and to learn to cope with difficulties resulting from the absence of their fathers, was evidence that the cultural script of the "all-important father" is a lie. These girls and their families had managed. On the other hand, their difficulties—emotional and financial, to name only two—and their lingering longings and resentments suggest that the cultural script of the "unimportant father" is equally a lie.

Faith of Our Fathers?

In the United States, girls today stand a far greater chance of sharing their religious involvements with their mothers than with their fathers. This assertion is simply the necessary result of the fact that churches in America attract significantly more women than men. Membership statistics in my denomination, for example—the Presbyterian Church (U.S.A.)—cite female members as composing 62 percent of total denominational membership, with some individual congregations having even higher numbers of women congregants.[6] The "feminization of religion" is not a new phenomenon. In terms of father-daughter relationships, however, a father's lack of shared faith perspectives with his daughter can pose some issues.

Leslie, as we saw earlier, managed to keep a close connection with her father despite his lack of involvement in the faith community that was so central to her. But a number of other girls who were my research partners at YTI found that their fathers' lack of faith created distance in their relationships with them.

Fathers might be surprised by daughters' efforts to understand their fathers' religious perspectives (or lack thereof). Jessica, for example, responded this way to a question about her father's religious beliefs:

> My dad does not like church, but he's religious. He's probably—he can probably tell you every verse in the Bible. But, um, church—some of the people drive him crazy. [*Laughter*.] I guess—I don't know if it's the hypoc—yeah, I think it's the hypocrisy. It drives him crazy. So he doesn't go to church except, maybe, if I'm [involved in a leadership role in the service] or—if I have something special, like—when we're confirmed, he goes. But that's about it. I always saw him as nonreligious until I started discussing things with him. Then I realized how much he really did know about it. And I think he tries to live his life.

So what is it that allows you to classify your dad as a religious person?

I guess just because he knows a lot about the Bible. . . . You know, he's a loving person, he tries to—I don't know—the way he lives his life, I guess.

Thus Jessica had to update her understanding of her father in light of the new depth of her discussions with him, which allowed her to view his stance toward the church differently from the way she had seen it before late adolescence.

Nevertheless, girls' ability to empathize with their fathers' choices about church participation did not translate into their feeling content with their fathers' different faith perspectives. Samantha, sixteen at the time of her interview, spoke with considerable understanding about her father's lack of religious involvement, yet she continued to wish he would "come to know God" because she believed that his doing so would change his life in positive ways. In other words, she wanted for her father what she herself had experienced through her faith:

I think my parents both are very good people. You know, they do a lot of great things for people that need it, and stuff like that. But um, my mom's different from my dad in that my mom—my mom loves going to church. She loves God very much. I talk to her about stuff, and things like that. And I think that—that God guides her in her decisions. Like, she listens to Him, where—I don't think my dad, like, gives a rip. . . . I think he believes in God. I know he believes in God. I know for a fact that he believes in God.

How do you know that?

[*Pause.*] I knew growing up that there was God, at home. I don't know how I knew, but I know that both of my parents believe in God. I don't even know how—I have no idea. But, um, my dad—he enjoys going to church when I go, and stuff like that. But it's just not a priority. It's not something he wants to do every week, or it's not something that he needs—*wants* to think about every day. And I can see that. Like, there are a lot of things about him that would be different if he knew God . . . the way other people do.

Like what?

Um, he's a real negative person. You know, he's a very helpful person, and he'll do a lot of things for other people, but he's just, um—he's very negative, and, um, nothing will ever turn out good, no matter what. Everything can be fine, he just has a very negative, negative

outlook on everything, and um—I don't know, he's just, like—he frus-
trates me a lot, like, the way that he talks, or the way that—I don't
know. I mean, he's a good guy, everyone is always saying what a great
guy he is, but he makes me mad, you know.

In addition to her perception that her father might be "different if he
knew God," Samantha articulated her sense that her father could not
really understand her or know her without grasping the significance of
her faith in her everyday life and relationships:

> *What would you like him to know about you, that you think he
> doesn't know?*
>
> Oh wow. Um—I think he, like—I'd want him to know the kind of. . . .
> [Pause.] I think I'd want him to know about, like, the things that I tell
> my really close friends. My friend that got me going to the church that
> I go to now—we talk all the time about, you know, what we've been
> praying about, and—and [Samantha's father] just doesn't understand
> that I make my decisions, or I try—that I should make my decisions
> by what God wants me to do. He just doesn't see that. He didn't
> understand why I wanted to come here [to YTI]. You know, he was
> just thinking about, I was going to be gone for a month. And, see,
> that's where it's hard, because I can't just be resentful toward my dad,
> because he was going to miss me very much, and that's why he didn't
> want me to come. And that's great! It's not that he's an unloving
> guy—he is, he's a great guy, and he wants me to be home for a month,
> and he misses me, and all. But he doesn't see why this is important in
> my relationship with God, why I needed to come.
>
> *He can't share that part of it with you?*
>
> Exactly.

Samantha's comments evidenced the longing seen among a number of
the girls in this interview group to share with their dads the faith that was
so important in their own lives. As was also true in the case of mothers
who did not profess the same beliefs as their daughters, this difference in
faith between fathers and daughters did not necessarily mean that the
nonbelieving or differently believing fathers could not support the spiritual lives of their believing daughters. Clearly, these girls would have felt
most supported if their fathers had been able to share the spiritual worldview that they themselves found so life-affirming. But, in the absence of
that option, their fathers could still affirm their daughters' participation
in religious communities as well as their daughters' efforts to live their

lives from a coherent practice of faith. These daughters desired their fathers' blessings on their religious involvements, even if their fathers did not share those involvements.

At the same time, girls for whom questions of faith were the most important ones to ponder felt acutely the limitations imposed on their relationships with their fathers by the fact that their fathers were people who never gave thought to such matters. Susan, for example, whose mother participated with her in their Presbyterian church and whose father was Jewish, did not expect her father to share her beliefs. What she wished for instead was that he would talk with her, from the perspective of his own tradition, about some of the "big questions" with which she was continually wrestling. Reflecting on this gap in her relationship with her father, she recalled:

> I asked [my dad] once, like, "What do you believe? Do you believe there's a God?" He's, like, well—like, "I guess there's got to be something—like, I've never really thought about it before." And I'm, like, "How do you never really think about it before?" You know, I just ponder these things for hours and hours.

Both Samantha and Susan commented that their fathers did go to church if their daughters had some important event happening there, and this was a fatherly gesture of obvious significance to these girls. Both also mentioned, with energy, their view of their fathers as good people who were living from values compatible with their daughters' faith perspectives. These girls may have wished for more support, or for support of a different kind, but they nevertheless did experience their dads' implicit support for their spiritual quests and practices, in the form of their fathers' openness to their daughters' active faith lives.

A nonbelieving father could still be supportive of the spiritual life of his daughter. But if he expressed total indifference or hostility to his daughter's beliefs, that behavior undoubtedly had a negative effect on the girl and on her relationship with him, as was also the case with nonbelieving mothers who behaved in this way. One girl spoke of her stepfather's active hostility to her religious practices:

> He says things like "Why do you have to be going to church all the time? Why can't you just pray at home and save your money? Do you think it makes you a better person than the rest of us?" I hate when he talks like that, like he holds me in disdain for believing in God.

Another noted sadly:

> My father won't even come to church if I am the preacher on youth
> Sunday, or if I play the prelude. It's sorta like that part of my life
> doesn't exist for him.

Thus a nonbelieving father's hostility or indifference can create a huge
barrier to his connection with his believing daughter, a barrier that sits
between them as a gaping wound that becomes increasingly resistant to
healing.

Fortunately, most of the girls in my interview group who talked about
marginally believing or nonbelieving dads, or about fathers who belonged
to other (non-Christian) faith traditions, had not experienced such hostility or indifference from their fathers. Instead, they and their fathers
appeared to be engaged in a kind of dance, each attempting to understand the other while maintaining his or her separate perspective. This
difference between them was sometimes upsetting and often frustrating
to the girls, but they saw it as yet another feature of the father-daughter
relationship that they needed to rework in adolescence.

Saying "Father," Meaning "God"

Talking with girls about their fathers and their religious beliefs in the
same conversation means that eventually the issue of using "father" language to speak about God will come to the fore. In Christian tradition,
the use of "Father" as a metaphor (or even a name) for God remains
common. In spite of several decades of work by feminists and progressive
Christians to expand God talk beyond the singular use of male, paternal
terms for God, "Father" remains the dominant way of referring to God
in many congregations and in American civil religion. When I asked girls
about the language they used to refer to God, they offered a wide variety
of responses, including "Father," "Mother," "Spirit," "Infinite Beauty,"
and "Loving Friend."

During some of the summer sessions at YTI, issues concerning gender
and God talk become hot topics. Does God have gender? What does it do
to God, and to us, when we use only male pronouns and terms to refer to
God? How might it enlarge the ways we understand God if we used
words other than "He" and "Father" to talk about or refer to God?
What meanings are contained in the term "Father" that are important to
maintain in talking about God in other terms? These are the kinds of
questions that YTI youth discuss as they wrestle with ancient and

contemporary theological ideas, and the same issues were often prominent in my interviews with girls.

Some girls had come to YTI fully aware of these issues; others were new to conversations about gender, God, and the power of language to limit human capacities for imagining God. Thus many of the girls in my interviews spoke of experimenting with new words for thinking about God and for addressing God in prayer. Elaine put it this way:

> I associate "He" with God, "Father" with God. But we've been talking about it a lot during this program, and I do agree that we shouldn't use only male words, because we are putting limits on Him, and He's limitless. Well, *God* is limitless, see? I did it—I said "He"! It's making me think, anyway. I always have associated a gender with Him—I mean, God—but I don't think there should be only one [gender identity associated with God].

Some girls did mention their efforts to think about God in terms of images that were not paternal, but they still usually addressed God in prayer as "Father." "It's a habit," was the oft-repeated refrain.

My listening to girls talk about their fathers and about their preferred terminology for God helped me see, in part, why this figure of speech is so resistant to change: it is an expression of the Ideal Father, a representation of a perfect father who loves unconditionally, exercises power beneficently and justice perfectly, protects without fail, and will never leave.[7] When these girls used the term "Father" to refer to God, they tapped into a deep well of emotion and desire about their own fathers.

Elaine, for example, whose relationship with her father was conflicted and tumultuous, had this to say:

> Basically, my image of God is [that of] a good father. I have replaced my father with God as a father figure because it helps me out, thinking of God as my father.

Carol, a Roman Catholic girl, echoed Elaine's words:

> I don't have a very good relationship with my father. I like to think that, yes, we all have a Father—you know, God—and if I could think that there still is one . . . you know what I'm saying—that maybe I don't have him in the physical being right in front of me [her father], but that there is one spiritually for me?

For these girls, the image of God as their Father functioned in a compensatory manner, to help them deal with the gap between their actual human fathers and the wished-for, idealized Father of their imaginations. But not all girls assumed that they could bridge the gaps in their relationships with their human fathers by depicting God as a perfect father. Some saw their painful relationships with their human fathers as a logical reason to leave behind the use of paternal imagery for God. Leslie, whose congregation regularly used gender-inclusive language for God, and who had obviously thought about these issues before coming to YTI, suggested that Christians should be more cautious in using "Father" to refer to God

> because I think it makes a lot of women uncomfortable, and anything that makes someone uncomfortable should be looked at very carefully. Also, because—to me, it limits who God is. If we say God is male, then isn't God also a mother, isn't God also female? It limits God too much to be one or the other.

Carol, who liked the idea that a Father-God could compensate for the failings of a human father, spoke about the pain she had experienced in her relationship with her father as she tried to deal with his excessive drinking. She recalled a time when, in the grip of an impulsive rage, he had struck her. She often prayed to God or to Jesus about ordinary matters, but when it came to her father's unpredictable temper, Carol usually prayed to Mary:

> I feel that she was a woman on earth who suffered a lot. To see your son persecuted on a daily basis, and the ultimate thing—being nailed to a cross, I mean, completely innocent! I know she really suffered, and I really feel like she knows what it means to suffer. She also knows what it means to—I guess I want to say, be kind of assumptioned [assumed] into heaven. We believe, as Catholics, that she was taken body and soul into heaven. So she knows—from every time I've suffered in my life, I've grown closer to God, and I feel she knows the same thing. I feel she knows the ultimate thing of suffering and yet receiving something really redeeming in the end.

Even with her compensatory notion of God as Father, Carol preferred to pray to the one she called "Mother" when dealing with suffering in her relationship with her dad.

Similarly, Kit asked:

> What if someone had been really, really hurt by their father—like, abused or abandoned, or something—and then the church tells them

that they have to call God "Father" if they want to talk to God, talk about God? It might be a big barrier for them. I think there must be more ways than just "Father" to say "God."

Indeed there are.

Great Fathers, Good Fathers, and Good-Enough Fathers

It was not only while using God talk that the girls in these interviews expressed their ideal visions of a father. Some girls used images from television and film to communicate how they viewed fatherhood. Mikela, for example, found a compelling image of a father in one of the characters from *The Cosby Show:*

> A good father is like Bill Cosby['s amiable character, Dr. Huxtable]. Well, not as perfect as him. But I guess someone who is loving, who is willing to admit their mistakes, who loves me—who's willing to be a good role model, who I know will be there when I need him—who will sacrifice for me, like my mother did.

Interestingly, in her final phrase, Mikela described her concept of a good father by naming something her mother had done for her—an implicit suggestion that what is important is a parent's actions or qualities, not the parent's gender.

Mary used a different figure from popular culture as a reference, pointing to the father in the John Hughes film *Sixteen Candles* because

> a good father is one that you [can] really talk to, and in the end, he was so understanding of his daughter.

The desire for an understanding dad was a major theme among these girls. Jennifer, for example, discussing her relationship with her father, indicated that the sense of being understood by her dad was even more important than the ability to share emotions with him. Asked about times when she had felt close to her father, she replied:

> Maybe not emotionally, because he's not an emotional person. But, um—I think, more than [with] my mom, I can probably share with him more, because he . . . it's not that my mom doesn't listen, it's just that I don't feel comfortable with, um . . . maybe I just don't feel comfortable with her. I mean, I don't share very deep emotional things with my dad, but I feel like I can carry on a conversation with my dad, and he knows exactly where I'm coming from. I feel like he cares

more, maybe. When we're with friends, or something, he always mentions things I've done, which kind of is annoying, but I appreciate it. Like, when I got here, he was talking to the director of YTI and saying, "She's been on two mission trips," and, you know, I'm kind of embarrassed—but I can tell he's proud of me. And that's important to me.

Jennifer clearly enjoyed her father's engaging in a little paternal boasting about her, even if it caused her a twinge of social embarrassment to listen in on such affirmations from her dad. Her father's words communicated, both to Jennifer and to others, that he saw and valued his daughter's activities—in this case, her participation in mission trips through their church. For Jennifer, the sense that her father cared about and understood her came through such public expressions of his pride in her. It was a way for him to bless her.

In fact, when Jennifer and other girls in the interview group described their own fathers as embodying the qualities of a good father, they were often referring to this practice of dads affirming their daughters to others. There are significant cultural and developmental reasons why practices of paternal affirmation become important. In a society driven by a market mentality, where self-promotion is the de facto norm, it remains para-doxically taboo to appear to be *explicitly* promoting oneself. Explicit self-affirmation is generally seen as narcissistic; at best, it is considered to be bragging or boasting, a type of socially unacceptable behavior.

And girls know this. Therefore, when an adolescent girl, whose sense of positive self-regard is very much under construction, has a parent who can speak well of her actions and her person without violating this code of modesty, she has an important resource. Such a parent allows her to benefit from hearing herself affirmed, from hearing her parent believe in her out loud. She can, in effect, borrow the regard in which her parent holds her as a source of strength until such time as this sense of self-affirmation becomes a part of her own internal understanding of herself.

Girls used words like "strong" and "protective" when describing their own fathers as well as their images of what constituted a good father. And quite a few of these girls, asked to describe a good father in general, responded by saying, "My dad—he's a good father." Andrea, for exam-ple, said:

I would actually picture my dad. There is absolutely nothing that he could have done any better for me. Because, like, anything that's important to me—he takes time out. He'll skip work, he'll do any-thing. When I was in junior high, he would drive up from work on his lunch break to eat lunch with me in the car. Just stuff like that—it seems so dumb, but it matters a lot to me.

Fathers who spent time with their daughters received big points in these girls' assessments of them. In many instances, girls identified this quality of fatherhood in explicit juxtaposition to images of fathers whose primary means of relating to their daughters was as financial providers. Brenda, an African American girl from the rural South, pointed to this distinction in her remarks:

> My image of a good father is one that spends time with his kids and is *there*—not just providing money and stuff, and providing, like, food and stuff, but providing love and attention. And going to ball games and dance recitals and, you know, awards banquets. Just being there—just to have Daddy around.

As noted earlier, such conversations show that many of these girls, in their relationships with their fathers, were perched on the edge of a major transformation in the role of fathers in family life in the United States. This transformation—from a paternal role defined primarily in terms of fathers' being financial providers to one defined by fathers' emotional involvement and participation in the experiential worlds of their children—meant that these girls generally had high expectations for their fathers to participate in their lives.[8] Such changes in fathering signal positive gains for daughters, who surely benefit from their fathers' greater emotional availability and more engaged parenting.

At the same time, however, such higher expectations—fleshed out by cultural fantasies of fatherhood and media images of wonderful, perfectly relational dads, and further buttressed by religious imagery of fatherly perfection—put a lot of pressure on fathers to be superhuman. It may be helpful if fathers, instead of cracking under the pressure, appropriate and adapt an idea about mothering that was introduced into psychology in 1971 by Donald W. Winnicott.[9] Winnicott surmised that babies need good mothers, but not necessarily perfect ones. In fact, a perfect mother may actually thwart the well-being of her child by depriving him or her of encounters with the normal frustrations that are necessary to childrens' growth and development. What is needed, Winnicott said, is not perfect mothering but good-enough mothering. Good-enough mothers allow enough challenge and frustration for babies to develop beyond their current abilities in order to cope effectively. But good-enough mothers also recognize what constitutes too much difficulty, and they endeavor to protect their babies from being overchallenged and overfrustrated in ways that do not promote growth. Perhaps in this age of fatherhood's transformation, Winnicott's idea can be applied to dads and pulled forward into the adolescent years of their children's lives.

A girl probably does not need a perfect father. She may not even need a great father. What she does need, and what her father realistically can become for her, is a father who is good enough—a father who is there for his daughter as the finite human being he is.

Reflections

One of the best contemporary studies on fathers I have seen is a book by John R. Snarey, *How Fathers Care for the Next Generation,* which begins with these words:

> This book is about good fathers. By good, I mean generative fathers: men who contribute to and renew the ongoing cycle of the generations through the *care* they provide as birth fathers (biological generativity), childrearing fathers (parental generativity), and cultural fathers (societal generativity).[10]

Across many centuries, fathers have provided these distinctive forms of care, in ways that have fit the cultures, contexts, and fathering norms of their times—which is to say, there have always been good fathers.

And there are good fathers today. Men tell me that it is extremely difficult to know just what fathering, much less good fathering, means right now, especially when children reach the teen years. Walking onto the terrain of father–adolescent girl relationships today seems a bit like taking a journey into uncharted territory where, you have been told, there "probably" is quicksand, so you need to keep walking, but be careful, for you will inevitably fall into it. For dads—some of whom are experimenting with or have already embraced new meanings for fatherhood, beyond those they experienced with their own fathers—there is no clear template to follow. Such an adventure can be very exciting. It is also extremely hard work, with uncertain support and sometimes, in the short term, relatively few visible rewards.

Listening to girl talk on fathers has helped me realize the variety of ways in which fathers matter in the lives of girls, as well as the many possibilities fathers have for supporting the religious lives of their daughters. Fathers support their daughters in many ways that ultimately contribute to their daughters' spiritual lives. They talk with their daughters about the important "big questions" in life. They share the significance of their work with their daughters. They just show up for their daughters' soccer games. They console their daughters over the loss of a big scholarship. And yet, in the midst of all these smaller actions, which communicate priorities and values and manifest a father's love, what strikes me is the overarching significance of one particular means of explicit spiritual support: namely, the power that fathers have to bless their daughters, not like the patriarchs of old, but in their role as contemporary fathers who have multiple ways to express their generative care. This power to bless can be life-changing and transformative, both for those who give and for those who receive the blessing.

6

GIRL TALK, GOD TALK

SOMETHING HAS BEEN ABSENT from contemporary efforts to know and understand the worlds of adolescent girls. Those efforts toward more complete knowledge have managed to get girls into the pages of textbooks on adolescent development. And studies of girls today offer new insights into everything from how girls fight to how girls learn in schools. We know more about the kinds of problems girls today experience—eating disorders, date rape, hidden depression, sexual harassment in schools, and, for some girls, the intersections of racism and class oppression with sexism. Out of that knowledge we are learning about how better to support girls and encourage their resilience in the face of such difficulties. And yet something is missing from much of the scholarly and popular literature on girls because these works, vital though they are, fail to give attention to the spiritual and religious lives of girls.

Ask girls about the times they feel most alive, and they will name experiences as wide-ranging as staying up all night talking with a best friend, dancing or listening to certain kinds of music, walking on the beach alone, participating in a huge national church youth event or in a massive antiwar protest, spending time with a boyfriend, accomplishing a goal on a mission trip, serving as a volunteer reader in the children's room of the library, and competing in a sports event. Press a little further, to explore what it is about these experiences that constitutes them as fully alive moments, and most girls engage in some kind of meaning making, placing the particular experience into a larger framework in order to understand it. Inside these specific experiences of aliveness for girls are the elements of compassion, integrity, vocation, and justice that comprise their spirituality.

Elements of Religious Life for Girls

Why are the religious lives of girls such key elements in understanding girls? In this book, by sharing the voices of girls talking about faith, gender, and family, I have suggested that in order to know girls, one has to understand the orienting worldview through which they make sense of their reality. Spirituality, or religion, involves a set of practices that simultaneously express meanings and shape particular worldviews. In other words, to speak of the religious lives of girls is not simply to catalogue certain religious activities that they perform, such as reading the Bible, worshiping with a faith community, or praying. That would be to treat spirituality as a kind of add-on to an existing self and life.

Spirituality emerges out of the combination of two interrelated aspects of experience. The first of these arises from the need to make sense of one's day-to-day life. It comes from being fully alive in the present, aware of one's experiences. For example, if I am walking on a beach, perhaps I notice the feeling of the sun and the wind on my skin. As I look out over the vastness of the sea, I may interpret my sensory experience in that moment merely as a pleasant set of sensations felt in a beautiful natural context. It is good to do that; one cannot live well if one is disengaged from the present moment and from one's experience of it.

But a second aspect of experience is that of transcendence. Human beings have the capacity to recognize that there is something bigger than ourselves. We make sense of our particularity in part by locating ourselves within something larger. So, walking on the beach, I may experience the sun's warmth and the wind's caressing sensations with pleasure while I also relate them to a sense of connection with the nonhuman creation. I may have an awareness of gratitude for being able to have such an experience, an awareness that leads me to express my thanks to the Creator in prayer. Or perhaps looking out over the horizon of the sea puts me in perspective as a rather small part of a much larger universe, with God larger still. I make sense of my physical sensations and my aesthetic enjoyment by understanding them in terms of God's creative activity and my relationship to the nonhuman creation and to God. This is no longer simply a jaunt down the beach. Rather, the moment takes on meaning as a time of communion with the Creator. The Christian view of God as Creator of the universe becomes the lens through which I make *different* sense of a walk on the beach.

Living the spiritual life means engaging in a way of being that holds together these two aspects of experience, the here and now and transcendence, in everyday practices and acts of making meaning. Adolescent girls are particularly well positioned to hold the tension between these two aspects of spirituality. Whether by social construction or biological factors, girls especially live in their bodies, highly aware of their own embodiment in all its immediacy. Furthermore, girls tend to place priority on relationships in ways that invite interconnection with their contexts—a certain consciousness of those around them. Thus they can be quite present to the situations, relationships, and contexts in which they find themselves. In short, gender positioning[1] locates, or situates, girls toward immanence.

At the same time, developmental features of adolescence mean that these girls have heightened capacities for imagining larger-than-self realities. Cognitive development in adolescence means that they have access to realms of the imaginary, the possible (in contrast to the merely actual), and the utopian that go beyond childhood capacities for thinking. The intensification of affect (the world of feelings) that these girls also experience, from the combination of their gender positioning and their adolescent development, means that they bring to their cognitive task of making meaning the additional power of feeling and desire that causes them to reach beyond themselves. Gender positioning and developmental change together move girls toward transcendence. In effect, girls are especially primed in adolescence to engage their spiritual resources across all aspects of their lives. In touch with the ordinary, and drawn toward transcendence, girls in the teen years have the potential to tap these spiritual resources, which can take them into a vigorous and meaningful young adult life. That recognition makes it rather surprising that scholars and writers focused on adolescent girls have so consistently ignored the religious elements of girls' experience. But adults who are attuned to spiritual life, and who care about girls, can do much to foster the faith of adolescent girls and in so doing contribute to their flourishing. The evidence for this claim comes from the voices of these girls, who have spoken about what it means to be young, female, and Christian today. What stands out most about what they have said? I want to underscore four key findings from my interviews with this group of girls:

1. Girls want adults as conversation partners and sponsors in their lives of faith.

2. Girls today continue to struggle with problematic gender oppression. Often they seem unaware of how they internalize this oppression and capitulate to restrictive gender roles. Christian spirituality can support the thriving of girls and their struggles for gender justice. In some forms, however, it can also be implicated in underwriting the

subordination of women. Girls need help sorting these issues out, and they need advocacy to help them resolve issues of gender justice in relation to faith.

3. Parents matter greatly in the religious lives of their daughters. Whether or not they intend to, they shape their daughters' spiritual lives in important ways.

4. Girls are active meaning makers in relation to faith. They value religious experience, and they want their faith to make a difference in their individual lives and in the larger world.

By way of conclusion, I will comment briefly on each of these findings.

Girls and Adult Conversation Partners

In a youth-oriented culture that focuses on the importance of the peer group for adolescents, it can seem that the only relevant or desirable people teens can talk with are other teens. Christian youth ministry models have bought into this notion by focusing almost all their attention on interactions in peer groups, often to the exclusion of meaningful relationships between teens and adults. It is true that the girls in these interviews liked interaction with their peers. In many different ways, however, they also said that they longed for adult faith mentors. They wanted mothers, fathers, and other adults in their lives to think critically with them about faith questions. They wanted to push—and have someone respectfully push back. They wanted to be able to ask "big questions" and search for meaning in the company of adults as well as in the company of their peers.

Such desires point to a form of learning and spiritual growth that is much like apprenticeship. Apprentices spend time in the presence of one who is a more seasoned practitioner of something that they wish to learn. Over time, the apprentice, by observing and sharing in the practices that make up the work to which she aspires, develops capacities for that work. Asking questions, and struggling with difficult problems in the company of someone who has a stake in the same issues (the master craftsperson, in this analogy), are also key to the experience of being "formed" in a way of life. In turn, those who help to bring newcomers into the practices that constitute their way of life find new growth and refreshment in their own experience through engagement with their apprentices.

What I heard these girls saying was that they were ready and willing to be spiritual apprentices, people active in the pursuit of spirituality through relationships with more seasoned practitioners of faith. The problem they named is that it was not always easy for them to find sponsors, adults who were willing to take on apprentices in religious life. Too often the girls' efforts to struggle with hard questions met pat answers or responses that seemed either simplistic or inauthentic. Their demands for religious talk to be matched by action were trivialized and disregarded as youthful idealism. This also permitted the girls' concerns for integrity to be disregarded rather than actively provoked by adult sponsors who could help them channel their longing for authenticity into forms of spiritual activism that would matter for the life of the world. In short, the girls identified a gap between their desire for adult faith mentors and the availability of such people in their lives.

This is a gap that those of us who care about the spiritual lives of adolescent girls can do something about. We can fill it by cultivating relationships with adults who can be mentors for our daughters. We can fill it by seeking out communities in which there are adults worthy of being apprenticed to in faith. Christian spirituality involves many individual practices and components, but ultimately it is a life best lived in a community of faith, where many others walk alongside one in the effort to live and practice one's faith. We can support the spiritual lives of girls by engaging in a faith community where people actively struggle to make sense of their everyday experience and to reach for the transcendent with authenticity and integrity.

The notion of apprenticeship depends on the presence of a seasoned practitioner, one who is experienced in practices of faith. Does that mean that parents have to have their own religious lives, ideas, and practices all worked out if they wish to support the spirituality of their teenage daughters? No, of course not. Sometimes young people who have had no direct religious upbringing or religious experience in their families begin as teens to cultivate their spiritual lives. Parents who did not attend to their daughters' religious lives in childhood may falsely believe that they have already missed the train. They may think they started paying attention to spirituality too late to have any impact on their daughters.

It is true that girls who have experienced a lifetime of immersion in a faith community and its traditions will come into adolescence with a different repertoire of resources, symbols, conversation partners, and knowledge from which to fashion their religious lives in adolescence. But the life of faith is dynamic, not static. There is a "start wherever you are" character to spirituality, a fluidity and an openness that allow for early starters and late bloomers. Even lifelong practitioners of faith, who have been intentional about nurturing the religious lives of their daughters from birth forward, still change and grow in their own faith. The season of their children's adolescence provides opportunities for adults to reopen and unsettle what has become closed and too settled in their own faith. This can happen as teens raise questions and doubts. It can even happen in the encounter with adolescent critiques of adult hypocrisy. An adolescent living with adults who are companions in the spiritual life, and who are still learning and developing their own practices, is provided with important and positive models and support for faith. Regardless of whether girls or adults or both are in the position of beginners, there are resources and support for fostering the spiritual life. And in a faith community, it need not all depend on parents. There are "other mothers" and "other fathers," perhaps more seasoned in their spiritual walks, who can be mentors to girls.

One concrete step adults can take is to nurture their own faith by reading, taking classes, or joining Bible-study groups. Adults can also learn about and try different forms of prayer, such as centering prayer or walking the labyrinth. Take some steps to practice Sabbath keeping. Go with your daughter to her place of worship, or find and try participating in a faith community that interests you. When your daughter is willing, discuss "big questions" with her to learn what she is passionate about and what she is thinking, and to discover how she is making religious sense of her experience. Sometimes this kind of discussion happens directly. Often, though, it may be indirect, in conversation about a film or events in the news.

Support your daughter's efforts to integrate her spiritual practices into the household. Some young women have absolutely no interest in doing this, but where there is any indication of interest, it is extremely supportive for girls to see that their families are willing to try something different in relation to faith practices. For example, one girl for whom creation care and ecospirituality were central wanted her family members to intensify their recycling practice and work to reduce household waste to one bag of trash per week. Her parents, not Christians themselves, were able to take these practices on in support of their daughter's spirituality even though they did not attribute the same theological meanings to their actions.

In some families, it may be possible to intentionally take on one or two small ritual elements that honor a girl's spiritual interests. For instance, in one family whose members did not all feel comfortable with the practice of praying a table grace, the parents responded to their daughter's wish to have at least some kind of prayer before meals when family members ate together by lighting a candle and observing a moment of silence before the start of the meal. Such microsteps may seem like gestures too small to matter, yet in efforts to foster the religious lives of girls, small gestures can be knit together to form a larger fabric of support.

Girls and Gender Oppression

For me, one of the most disturbing aspects of these interviews concerned the continuing power of sexism to get inside the skins and minds of girls, problematically shaping their perceptions and practices of female gender identity. I was surprised and disturbed to learn of the extent to which some girls still capitulated to negative or trivializing understandings of what it means to be female, perspectives that required them to "de-self" or deny their own personhood. In several instances, their faith communities partici- pated in this oppression by authorizing it with interpretations of scripture or uses of religious tradition that encouraged women's subordination.

At the same time, though, this group of girls included those for whom Christian faith offered a different vision of what it means to be female. These girls participated in communities in which the meanings of gender did not include any notions of the "natural" subordination of women to men. For these young women, faith and Christian spirituality were ways of living in freedom, not oppression. They had already had opportunities to reflect on the different meanings given to gender, and to examine expe- riences of affirmation and discrimination related to being female.

What is clear from the interviews is that girls still need help sorting out the many conflicting messages about gender. Because so much about gen- der identity is tacit—just a part of who they are, like the air they breathe— it goes unexamined and unnoticed unless something happens to provoke attention to it. Adults who want to foster the spiritual lives of adolescent girls can provide occasions for bringing gender issues from tacit to explicit levels of awareness, by reflecting on media treatments of women and men, by processing the ideas and experiences girls share, and by reflecting with them on the various meanings attributed to being female and on issues of gender justice.

Some girls found strong role models among women in their faith com- munities. People in these congregations did not have to have their act completely together, in terms of eradicating all inconsistencies regarding gender issues, before the girls could recognize women leaders who offered alternatives to negative or restrictive meanings of being female. Neverthe- less, it is clear that when a faith community sends conflicting messages about women, those messages complicate a girl's experience and participa- tion if she is critically reflective about such matters. Therefore, an impor- tant attribute of adults who care about the spiritual lives of girls is the willingness to be present and to help girls navigate the faith community while also critiquing its problematic gender-related ideas and practices.

Girls and Their Parents

As is clear from girl talk on mothers and fathers, parents play a leading role in the religious lives of girls. They model values, virtues, and commitments. They show through their own work and life energies a sense of purposive vocation that becomes an important aspect of girls' spirituality. They participate in the development of empathy and compassion in their daughters. They demonstrate what forgiveness looks like, along with what it means to need to be forgiven. In other words, they are less than perfect!

Adolescent girls are active makers of meaning. They are shapers of faith practices. This reality works against any notion that a vital, healthy spirituality can be formed only in girls from "perfect" family situations and households. For one thing, these so-called perfect households seem to be in short supply. We are probably better off striving to be good-enough households in which parents generally are doing the best they can under what are inevitably less than perfect circumstances.

Furthermore, sometimes strengths emerge out of challenges. Parents certainly do not need to go out of their way to try to create negative or difficult experiences, which will come along on their own anyway; as active constructors of meaning, adolescent girls can make use of both a *via negativa* and times of harmony and well-being to shape a spiritual life. I can say this with confidence because what the girls in my interview conversations so poignantly illustrated is that they used whatever experiences they had in life as raw material for their spiritual reflections and practice.

Parents, of course, would wish that their messy divorce had not created pain or disillusionment in their daughter, but those parents need not worry that somehow the experience has kept their daughter from vibrant spirituality as an adolescent. Girls make meaning of all kinds of experiences that come their way. In fact, fathers and mothers do influence the faith practices of their adolescent daughters, whether or not they do so intentionally, because these girls make use of all the experiences and resources in their worlds to make religious meaning and shape practices of faith.

Parents can support the spiritual lives of their daughters by engaging in the work of healing where there has been pain or brokenness. They can seek out pastoral counselors or therapists who can help them identify and develop family or personal strengths and work through wounds. They can use the stories and symbols of the faith to help gain perspective or make sense of hard things. One family with an adopted daughter entered rocky shoals when she arrived at midadolescence, because of the intensity of her identity questions related to her adoption. This family began to engage the Christian perspective of all persons having been adopted by God. The girl's parents also retrieved part of their own story—their years of longing for a child, and their joy in their daughter's long-awaited arrival when they adopted her—and connected it to biblical stories of adoption, waiting, and being chosen. Their retelling of this story in relation to Christian symbols did not magically fix their daughter's struggles, but it did offer an alternative faith narrative for making sense of adoption and identity, one that supported her while she dealt with her questions.

Nurturing the faith practices of girls in situations of pain or stress can include supporting their participation in something beyond themselves and their difficulties. For many girls, going on a youth group's mission trip, or engaging in community service through school or church, can be a helpful reminder that others also struggle with life's difficulties. Getting active reminds young people that they are not totally helpless or powerless to change anything but in fact can act with meaning and purpose in the world. Encouraging their increasing capacity for empathy and their desire for even one small corner of the world to be better, by supporting them in taking action related to the causes they care about, can nurture girls' spiritual practices of compassion and justice.

In some situations, girls prefer to be on their own or with their friends in such activities. When a girl is open to it, however, participating with her parents in practices of service and care for others can be life-giving for all concerned.

Adults can also engage in the practice of contemplative listening, described earlier in this book (see Chapters One and Three). Listening with openness to a girl's experience of pain can be challenging, especially if an adult listener feels indicted or somehow responsible for the hurt. A posture of contemplative listening involves the listener's openness to the experiences, thoughts, and feelings of another—in this case, the adolescent girl. One listens for the metaphors and images that she uses to make sense of her experiences.

Girls as Makers of Meaning

At every turn, these girls spoke of the importance of authenticity in religion. They evoked religious life not simply as an idea but as something to be experienced. They were largely reluctant to use the term "religious" in describing themselves, and their reluctance concerned this issue of authenticity: girls were averse to allowing contemporary popular culture's meanings of religion to define their experience, religious and otherwise, and their way of life. Their general preference for the term "spiritual" must be seen not as a denigration of religion per se but in light of how important an experienced, authentic faith was for them. Parents and other adults can foster the spiritual lives of girls by inviting them to explore the various forms of language they use to express their spirituality, and to name what is most important in that language. We can be open to the meanings girls seek to convey with their choices of terms, even when some of those terms may seem not to refer to anything recognizably religious.

Because the spirituality of adolescent girls gives such priority to integrity between actions and beliefs or commitments, one important way that adults can nurture the faith of girls is to work at such authenticity and integrity themselves. They can also call their daughters to account when their daughters' actions contradict the values and religious meanings the girls hold.

When speaking of mothers and fathers alike, girls named the ways their parents' work had influenced their own vocational quests. They took pride in the kinds of work their parents did, or in perceptions of quality and of work well done. Girls, too, want their lives to matter in the world, and they see their future work as an important site for making a difference. Adults can support the spiritual lives of girls by supporting their vocational quests. They can talk with them about the values and commitments expressed in particular forms of work, and about the conflicts and problems, too.

Girls in this interview group experienced hopefulness and a sense of purpose when they participated in offering service to others. This practice is foundational for Christian spirituality, and the point bears repeating: one key way that adults can foster girls' religious lives is to affirm, support, and participate with them in practices of serving others.

Seasons of Life, Seasons of Parenting

For girls, the season of life known as adolescence is a particularly verdant one for spiritual growth and religious life. Parenting, too, has its seasons. In the season of parenting that includes adolescent children, parents have opportunities to consider and intentionally claim activities of faithful parenting that support the vitality of girls and their spiritual practices of compassion, integrity, vocation, and justice. In such an endeavor, this season of parenting may be one of growth for parents as well as for girls. After all, girls have a marvelous way of engaging in God talk in relation to practically every aspect of life. If we listen well to them, maybe we can learn to do that, too.

APPENDIX

RIVER OF LIFE:
A LIFE-REVIEW ACTIVITY

Instructions: This activity is designed to help you reflect on your life and tell your story.[1] It may be shared with another person or group or kept for personal reflection.

Begin with a blank sheet of paper. Before you put anything on the paper, think briefly about the course of your whole life. If you were to compare your life with a river, what would that river look like? When and where are the smooth, flowing waters—those times when events and relationships seem generally positive or there is a sense of ease about your life? When does the river take a sudden turn (and what caused the turn), or change from smooth waters to rough, tumbling rapids or to an excited rush of water? Are there rocks or boulders falling into your river—unexpectedly landed there, changing its direction forever? Are there points at which it flows powerfully and purposefully or seems to slow to a trickle?

A. Draw your river of life with its bends and turns, its smooth waters and rough spots, its strength/vitality, and its direction. Write in your approximate age, and/or the dates, along the flow of your river. Identify on your drawing the various key "marker events" in your life—the boulders in the river, or places where the river changes course, that shape your story. If you were to divide your life journey into sections, where would the section divisions occur? Give names to each of the sections of your life river.

B. Now think about the various people who have accompanied you along this river's journey. What relationships have been most significant at different points in your life? Who has most shaped you? Have there been significant losses of relationship along the way? What groups or communities of people were most important? Record these key relationships and losses in the appropriate places on your river of life. If you wish, you might also want to jot down some of the thoughts and feelings that go along with these relationships.

C. As you look over the diagram of your life river, think about the different ways you have experienced and understood God across your life. Who or what was God to you at the different times depicted in your diagram? What caused you to feel closer to, or more distant from, God at these different times? What places or situations were encounters with the Sacred for you? Have you faced situations or experiences devoid of any sense of God/the Sacred? Decide on a way to note these matters, with words and/or symbols, and place them into your diagram.

D. Are there times of significant pain or suffering—yours or others'—that shape the flow of your life river? What has happened along the journey of your life that you associate with evil?

E. Rivers do not exist in isolation but are always part of a larger ecology. So too is human life situated in a larger world. What was going on in the world—local, regional, and world events—that shaped the flow of your life river? Using words and/or symbols, place these events in the appropriate locations on your diagram.

F. What values, commitments, causes, or principles were most important to you at a given point in your life? Toward what goals, if any, were your primary energies directed—or, metaphorically speaking, what purposes and ends helped to shape the flow of life waters at a given time in your experience? Note these on your river diagram.

As you finish depicting your river of life, take a look over the whole diagram. Do its symbols and words seem to portray how you think and feel about the whole of your life? Is here some important element left out? Make adjustments as needed. Remember that no diagram can possibly capture all that shapes a person's journey. This tool is intended to be a beginning point for reflection and/or conversation, not a comprehensive depiction of your life!

NOTES

INTRODUCTION

1. The term "other mother" refers to an adult (a neighbor, an aunt, a family friend) who is not someone's biological mother but who is nevertheless in a mothering relationship with that person. I heard this and similar terms used by some girls, particularly African Americans, in their interviews. But the phrase first came to my attention in Patricia Hill Collins, *Black Feminist Thought: Knowledge, Consciousness, and Empowerment* (Boston: Unwin Hyman, 1990).

2. The Youth Theological Initiative is a Lilly Endowment–supported program focused on youth, theology, and public life. Every summer since 1993, the program has been held at the Candler School of Theology, on the campus of Emory University. The focus of YTI is public theology—that is, the connections between theology and such matters of public concern as urban homelessness, racial justice, environmental policy, and health care. The interviews that form the basis of this book were conducted between 1993 and 2000. In addition to those interviews I personally conducted, I am grateful to other researchers at YTI who engaged in this research with skill and sensitivity, including Karen DiNicola, Michael Hryniuk, Katherine Turpin, David White, and Dori Grinenko Baker.

3. Sharon Daloz Parks, *Big Questions, Worthy Dreams: Mentoring Young Adults in Their Search for Meaning, Purpose, and Faith* (San Francisco: Jossey-Bass, 2000).

4. Christian Smith and Melinda Lundquist Denton, *Soul Searching: The Religious and Spiritual Lives of American Teenagers* (New York: Oxford University Press, 2005).

5. Daniel J. Kindlon, *Alpha Girls: Understanding the New American Girl and How She Is Changing the World* (Emmaus, Pa.: Rodale, 2006).

6. Norine G. Johnson, Michael C. Roberts, and Judith Worell (eds.), *Beyond Appearance: A New Look at Adolescent Girls* (Washington, D.C.: American Psychological Association, 1999), 45.

7. Denise M. DeZolt and Mary Henning-Stout, "Adolescent Girls' Experiences in School and Community Settings," in ibid., 266.

8. For examples, see Dori Grinenko Baker, *Doing Girlfriend Theology: God-Talk with Young Women* (Cleveland: Pilgrim Press, 2005); Patricia H. Davis, *Counseling Adolescent Girls* (Minneapolis: Fortress Press, 1996); Smith and Denton, *Soul Searching*; Evelyn L. Parker, *Trouble Don't Last Always: Emancipatory Hope Among African American Adolescents* (Cleveland: Pilgrim Press, 2003); Evelyn L. Parker, *The Sacred Selves of Adolescent Girls: Hard Stories of Race, Class, and Gender* (Cleveland: Pilgrim Press, 2007); Dori Grinenko Baker and Joyce Mercer, *Lives to Offer: Accompanying Youth on Their Vocational Quests* (Cleveland: Pilgrim Press, 2007); and Barbara J. Blodgett, *Constructing the Erotic: Sexual Ethics and Adolescent Girls* (Cleveland: Pilgrim Press, 2002).

9. This information is based on data about parents' educational attainments and occupations and comes from my own analysis rather than from the self-identifications of the girls themselves. Class is difficult to define and multiple in character. I understand class as an identity rather than a fixed category, and consequently see it as a contributing aspect of the identities of all of these girls. In the U.S. context, where the myth of a "classless" society prevails, it is common for people of various class identities to name themselves as middle class and to treat class as a category relevant only for those who fall at the extremes of income (such as poor persons who are homeless and extremely wealthy persons). While I consider class to be a significant and fluid aspect of identity among the girls at YTI, the scope of this book and limitations of the interviews do not allow me to give it more central attention.

10. See American Association of University Women, *Shortchanging Girls, Shortchanging America: A Call to Action* (Washington, D.C.: American Association of University Women, 1991).

11. Patricia Tetlin. Minnesota Women's Fund, *Reflections of Risk: Growing Up Female in Minnesota: A Report on the Health and Well-Being of Adolescent Girls in Minnesota* (Minneapolis: Minnesota Women's Fund, 1990), 10.

12. Mary Bray Pipher, *Reviving Ophelia: Saving the Selves of Adolescent Girls* (New York: Putnam, 1994).

13. Lyn Mikel Brown and Carol Gilligan, *Meeting at the Crossroads: Women's Psychology and Girls' Development* (Cambridge, Mass.: Harvard University Press, 1992); Carol Gilligan, Janie Ward, Jill McLean Taylor, and Betty Bardige (eds.), *Mapping the Moral Domain: A Contribution of Women's Thinking to Psychological Theory and Education* (Cambridge, Mass.: Center for the Study of Gender Education and Human Development,

Harvard University Graduate School of Education, 1988); and Carol Gilligan, Nona Lyons, Trudy J. Hanmer, and Emma Willard School, *Making Connections: The Relational Worlds of Adolescent Girls at Emma Willard School* (Troy, N.Y.: Emma Willard School, 1989).

14. This topic is addressed by various chapters in Bonnie J. Ross Leadbeater and Niobe Way (eds.), *Urban Girls: Resisting Stereotypes, Creating Identities* (New York: New York University Press, 1996), especially Chapter Three.

15. See Kindlon, *Alpha Girls.*

CHAPTER 1: GIRL TALK

1. The Youth Theological Initiative's interview database contains transcripts of several hundred interviews with girls. Out of this large group I selected a set of fifty interviews to study for this book, basing my choices on the strong presence in the interviews of my central research themes of gender, faith, and family relationships.

2. See Sara Lawrence-Lightfoot and Jessica Hoffmann Davis, *The Art and Science of Portraiture* (San Francisco: Jossey-Bass, 1997).

3. Dori Grinenko Baker and Joyce Mercer, *Lives to Offer: Accompanying Youth on Their Vocational Quests* (Cleveland: Pilgrim Press, 2007).

4. Fowler's exercise and instructions for completing it can be found in James W. Fowler, *Faith Development and Pastoral Care* (Philadelphia: Fortress Press, 1987), 121–125. Over time, I developed an adaptation of this tool for use with girls, replacing the formal, linear chart format of Fowler's exercise with a flowing diagram that incorporates pictures and symbols as well as words, and that uses the metaphor of a "river of life" to invite reflection on life journeys; see the Appendix in this book.

CHAPTER 2: GIRL TALK ON FAITH

1. Throughout this book when I quote girls, I use the terms they have chosen, including their use of male pronouns for God, or gender-specific terms such as "man" to refer to humanity. In keeping with this practice, where girls have referred to God unquestioningly with the third-person male pronoun "He," I maintain the common practice of capitalizing this pronoun. I believe that doing so keeps faith with the perspectives rendered by the girls, and I therefore maintain this nomenclature even though it would not be my preferred way to write.

2. Girls like Dominique bring to the Youth Theological Initiative a sophisticated vocabulary and way of thinking that frequently makes its way into
their interviews. Dominique used the term "anthropomorphic" to refer
to the practice of characterizing divinity with human qualities. This reference followed an interesting conversation, earlier in her interview, about
Ebonics (African American dialects) and the problems that her extensive
vocabulary sometimes caused her as she sought to fit in with African
American peers who called her an "Oreo" (black on the outside, white on
the inside).

3. This perspective appeared to represent a shift for several girls in my interview group, for whom a more rule-bound, moralistic understanding of faith
had been the norm until quite recently. On the one hand, this shift may
have been related to the developments in critical thinking and capacity for
relationship that grow in later adolescence. On the other hand, however,
such changes may also have reflected the influence of exposure to difference. In widening circles of religious discourse and action (such as are
found through participation in the Youth Theological Initiative summer
academy), a more exclusively "personal" articulation of faith often begins
to open one up to faith's public, social dimensions.

4. Christian Smith and Melinda Lundquist Denton, *Soul Searching: The
Religious and Spiritual Lives of American Teenagers* (New York: Oxford
University Press, 2005), 27.

5. James W. Fowler's faith-development research helpfully identifies distinctions
among beliefs, religion, and faith. Religion, Fowler says, citing
W. C. Smith (Wilfred Cantwell Smith, *The Meaning and End of Religion*
[New York, Macmillan 1963]), consists of "cumulative traditions," that
is, particular symbols, stories, and artifacts expressing people's relationship to the sacred. Beliefs are certain ideas that are held. Faith, in contrast,
reflects "the person's or group's way of responding to the sacred as mediated
through the forms of the cumulative tradition. In this sense, faith is the per-
sonal appropriation of relatedness to the transcendent"; see James W. Fowler,
*Stages of Faith: The Psychology of Human Development and the Quest for
Meaning* (San Francisco: HarperOne, 1981), 9; and James W. Fowler,
"Faith/Belief," in Rodney J. Hunter (ed.), *Dictionary of Pastoral Care and
Counseling* (Nashville: Abingdon Press, 1990), 394. Faith is "at once
deeper and more personal than religion" (Fowler, *Stages of Faith*, 9).
Fowler views faith as a "dynamic pattern of trust and loyalty" potential in
all persons; that is, faith is a human quality or capacity. As Parks helpfully
puts it, faith is "the continual activity of composing meaning"; see Sharon

Daloz Parks, *The Critical Years: Young Adults and the Search for Meaning, Faith, and Commitment* (San Francisco: HarperOne, 1986), 31.

6. The sense of these girls' use of "spiritual" strikes me as similar to that of the notion of "religionless Christianity" described by neo-orthodox theologians such as Bonhoeffer in the mid-twentieth century; see Dietrich Bonhoeffer, *Letters and Papers from Prison* (London: SCM Press, 1953). These theologians wanted to critique cultural domestications of religion in which Christian religion came to be easily identified with certain social, political, and cultural movements (including Hitler's Nazi Party). Similarly, the girls I interviewed often seemed to use the term "religion" to refer to certain tacitly assumed popular-culture notions of faith.

7. See Fowler, *Stages of Faith*, 179; Robert Kegan, *The Evolving Self: Problem and Process in Human Development* (Cambridge, Mass.: Harvard University Press, 1982), especially 223–229; and Parks, *The Critical Years*, 76–85.

8. Émile Durkheim, *The Elementary Forms of the Religious Life* (New York: Free Press, 1965).

9. The sociologist Pierre Bourdieu, *The Logic of Practice* (Cambridge: Polity Press/Basil Blackwell, 1990), suggests that this "misrecognition" of the constitutive role of society in generating particular practices is a necessary part of the reproduction of culture. Developmentalists, by contrast, would undoubtedly note the tendency to ignore the roles of other people or forces (parents, religious traditions, and the like) in the shaping of practices as a part of adolescent development in which the locus of authority and identity shifts from external to internal sources.

10. According to Wade Clark Roof and William McKinney, *American Mainline Religion: Its Changing Shape and Future* (New Brunswick, N.J.: Rutgers University Press, 1987), 133, "The conservative religious presence in the media and their direct involvement in the political process serve to heighten public awareness of [what Martin Marty calls a 'seismic shift'] in American religion."

11. Walter Brueggemann, "Covenanting as Human Vocation," *Interpretation,* 1979, *33*(2), 126.

12. Walter Brueggemann, *Texts Under Negotiation: The Bible and Postmodern Imagination* (Minneapolis: Fortress Press, 1993), 12–13.

CHAPTER 3: GIRL TALK ON GENDER

1. Joan Jacobs Brumberg, *The Body Project: An Intimate History of American Girls* (New York: Vintage Books, 1998), 29.

2. Susan Bordo, in her work on anorexia and bulimia, offers the useful reminder that this preoccupation with thinness is not a simple matter of arbitrary media images but requires deeper cultural analysis that attends to the "intersection of culture with family, economic and historical developments, and psychological constructions of gender"; see Susan Bordo, *Unbearable Weight: Feminism, Western Culture, and the Body* (Berkeley: University of California Press, 1993), 33. She points out, for example, anorexia's association with affluence and the tendency to overlook genuinely overweight women in discussions of body-image problems. The complexity of body image as an issue of cultural (re)production helps explain, then, why women who become aware of the influence of media images on their own body consciousness cannot simply turn those influences off as they might turn off the television.

3. For example, 9.1 percent of European American girls in a study by the Melpomene Institute said they felt attractive or very attractive, compared to 40.0 percent of African American girls; see Lynn Jaffee and Judy Mahle Lutter, "Adolescent Girls: Factors Influencing Low and High Body Image,"*Melpomene Journal*, 1995, *14*(2), 14–22. See also Sumru Erkut, Jacquiline P. Fields, Rachel Sing, and Fern Marx, "Diversity in Girls' Experiences: Feeling Good About Who You Are," in Bonnie J. Ross Leadbeater and Niobe Way (eds.), *Urban Girls: Resisting Stereotypes, Creating Identities* (New York: New York University Press, 1996); and Janie Victoria Ward, "Raising Resisters: The Role of Truth Telling in the Psychological Development of African American Girls," pp. 85–99 in Leadbeater and Way (eds.), *Urban Girls*.

4. American Association of University Women, *Shortchanging Girls, Shortchanging America: A Call to Action* (Washington, D.C.: American Association of University Women, 1991).

5. Ward, "Raising Resisters," 89.

6. Erkut, Fields, Sing, and Marx, "Diversity in Girls' Experiences," 61.

7. Ibid.

8. Brumberg, *The Body Project*, xvii.

9. Ibid., xxi.

10. Ibid., 97.

11. By "gender identity," I mean a person's internalized sense of gender—the "fit" a person feels between his or her identity as a person or self and his or her ways of expressing and experiencing who he or she is as a gendered person. One of the difficulties many girls and women experience in negotiating gender identity today comes as their felt, lived experiences of who they are

bump up against contradictory expectations from the wider culture about what a woman is and does.

12. Drucilla Cornell, for example, refers to the "cultural fantasies" that shape how various differences are constructed in a given society, differences that include race, gender, and disability. These "fantasies" are unconsciously held notions that operate at the level of culture. See Drucilla Cornell, *Transformations: Recollective Imagination and Sexual Difference* (New York: Routledge, 1993).

13. Sandra Lee Bartky, *Femininity and Domination: Studies in the Phenomenology of Oppression* (New York: Routledge, 1990).

14. American Psychological Association Task Force on the Sexualization of Girls, *Report of the American Psychological Association Task Force on the Sexualization of Girls* (Washington, D.C.: American Psychological Association, 2007).

CHAPTER 4: GIRL TALK ON MOTHERS

1. Mary Bray Pipher, *Reviving Ophelia: Saving the Selves of Adolescent Girls* (New York: Putnam, 1994).

2. Lyn Mikel Brown, *Girlfighting: Betrayal and Rejection Among Girls* (New York: New York University Press, 2003).

3. Daniel N. Stern, *The First Relationship: Infant and Mother* (Cambridge, Mass.: Harvard University Press, 2002).

4. See Dori Grinenko Baker and Joyce Mercer, *Lives to Offer: Accompanying Youth on Their Vocational Quests* (Cleveland: Pilgrim Press, 2007).

5. See, for example, Raymond Montemayor, "Family Variation in Parent-Adolescent Storm and Stress," *Journal of Adolescent Research*, 1986, *1*, 15–31.

6. G. Stanley Hall, *Adolescence* (New York: Arno Press, 1969; originally published 1904).

7. Pipher, *Reviving Ophelia*, 103–104.

8. Janet Surrey, "The Mother-Daughter Relationship: Themes in Psychotherapy," in Janneke van Mens-Verhulst, Karlein Schreurs, and Liesbeth Woertman (eds.), *Daughtering and Mothering: Female Subjectivity Re-analyzed* (New York: Routledge, 1993).

9. Ana Mari Cauce, Yumi Hiraga, Diane Graves, Nancy Gonzales, Kimberly Ryan-Finn, and Kwai Grove, "African American Mothers and Their Adolescent Daughters: Closeness, Conflict, and Control," in Bonnie J. Ross Leadbeater and Niobe Way (eds.), *Urban Girls: Resisting Stereotypes, Creating Identities* (New York: New York University Press, 1996).

10. Lyn Mikel Brown and Carol Gilligan, *Meeting at the Crossroads: Women's Psychology and Girls' Development* (Cambridge, Mass.: Harvard University Press, 1992).

11. Carol Gilligan and Annie Rogers, "Reframing Daughtering and Mothering: A Paradigm Shift in Psychology," in van Mens-Verhulst, Schreurs, and Woertman (eds.), *Daughtering and Mothering*, 131.

12. Terri Apter, *Altered Loves: Mothers and Daughters During Adolescence* (New York: St. Martin's Press, 1990).

13. Elizabeth Debold, Lyn Mikel Brown, Susan Weseen, and Geraldine Kearse Brookins, "Cultivating Hardiness Zones for Adolescent Girls: A Reconceptualization of Resilience in Relationships with Caring Adults," in Norine G. Johnson, Michael C. Roberts, and Judith Worell (eds.), *Beyond Appearance: A New Look at Adolescent Girls* (Washington, D.C.: American Psychological Association, 1999).

14. Apter, *Altered Loves*, 112.

CHAPTER 5: GIRL TALK ON FATHERS

1. Margaret Atwood, *Cat's Eye* (New York: Anchor Books, 1998), 183.

2. In these accounts, fathers are credited with influencing everything from a girl's future success in her job or career to her sexual orientation and future marital happiness. Fathers undoubtedly do make distinctive contributions to their daughters' lives, but I am inclined to understand these largely as products of social positioning rather than as fixed characteristics ascribable to fathers per se. For example, it is known that a father's level of involvement with his children correlates positively with their future economic, educational, and social well-being. Advocates of conservative family policy interpret such correlations as resulting from certain supposedly natural and necessary links between fathers as males and the kinds of roles fathers play in some families in American society (such as the roles of breadwinner and provider). These advocates would claim that a man's "natural" role as the conduit to the world outside the home, and as the family's provider, positions him to make the distinctive contribution of enabling his children's greater future success in the workplace. Critical culture theorists interpret quite differently the relationship between a father's involvement and the future economic success of his children. They critique the idea that men's navigation of the larger world beyond the domestic arena on behalf of their children is a natural, fixed aspect of maleness, and they attribute any tendency toward this effect (for it is not a given) to society's structuring of gender and

class relationships in such a way that men have greater earning power than women, who continue to hold primary responsibility for the home and for child care. In other words, distinctions obviously exist between what fathers and mothers contribute to their families, but I am reluctant to attribute such distinctions to any fixed characteristics of gender per se rather than to the ways our society shapes gender differences in parenting.

3. Ralph LaRossa, *The Modernization of Fatherhood: A Social and Political History* (Chicago: University of Chicago Press, 1997), 14.

4. Ibid., 11.

5. Rachel Devlin, *Relative Intimacy: Fathers, Adolescent Daughters, and Postwar American Culture* (Chapel Hill: University of North Carolina Press, 2005).

6. Data from Research Services, Presbyterian Church (U.S.A.), *A Presbyterian Panel Snapshot: Characteristics of Presbyterians, 2005*, online at http://www.pcusa.org/research/panel/bg-snapshot-2005.pdf (retrieved September 7, 2007).

7. For a more detailed account of the connections between idealized father images and God, see Joyce Ann Mercer, "Psychoanalysis, Parents, and God: Julia Kristeva on the Imaginary Father and Subjectivity,"*Pastoral Psychology*, 2002, *50*(4), 243–258.

8. William Bradford Wilcox, *Soft Patriarchs, New Men: How Christianity Shapes Fathers and Husbands* (Chicago: University of Chicago Press, 2004), discusses the role of religion in the contemporary reshaping of fatherhood that I, along with the girls in my research, give witness to here. Wilcox, a sociologist, examines both conservative Protestant and mainline Protestant Christianity in the United States for its effects on fathers. He finds that conservative Christianity fosters and reinforces a more expressive, involved paternal role, in spite of its historical affirmation of gender-prescribed roles for father and mother that place fathers largely outside the home as breadwinners while mothers take primary responsibility for the care and nurturing of children. Wilcox notes that fathers' contributions to the well-being of women and children in families may be seen in positive associations between paternal presence and economic, educational, and emotional health of other family members (p. 6). He then considers the impact of men's religious participation on shaping the kinds of fatherhood they live out in their families.

9. D. W. Winnicott, *Playing and Reality* (New York: Basic Books, 1971).

10. John R. Snarey, *How Fathers Care for the Next Generation: A Four-Decade Study* (Cambridge, Mass.: Harvard University Press, 1993), 1.

CHAPTER 6: GIRL TALK, GOD TALK

1. I use the term "gender positioning" to refer to the way women are situated, or positioned, by the meanings given to being female. Although these meanings certainly deserve close scrutiny and critique for the problematic power arrangements they can involve, here I am merely taking at face value that girlhood and womanhood, in the current U.S. context, include, among other attributed meanings, those of relationality, social awareness of others, and close identification of selfhood with the body.

APPENDIX: RIVER OF LIFE: A LIFE-REVIEW ACTIVITY

1. This term and the categories found in A-F in the "River of Life" exercise are drawn from Fowler's "Tapestry of My Life," on which my "River" activity is based. I am grateful to him for permission to place his insights into a new form.

BIBLIOGRAPHY

American Association of University Women. *Shortchanging Girls, Shortchanging America: A Call to Action*. Washington, D.C.: American Association of University Women, 1991.

—— and Greenberg-Lake: The Analysis Group. *Shortchanging Girls, Shortchanging America: Executive Summary: A Nationwide Poll That Assesses Self-Esteem, Educational Experiences, Interest in Math and Science, and Career Aspirations of Girls and Boys Ages 9–15*. Washington, D.C.: American Association of University Women, 1994.

American Psychological Association Task Force on the Sexualization of Girls. *Report of the American Psychological Association Task Force on the Sexualization of Girls*. Washington, D.C.: American Psychological Association, 2007.

Apter, Terri. *Altered Loves: Mothers and Daughters During Adolescence*. New York: St. Martin's Press, 1990.

Atwood, Margaret. *Cat's Eye*. New York: Anchor Books, 1998.

Baker, Dori Grinenko. *Doing Girlfriend Theology: God-Talk with Young Women*. Cleveland: Pilgrim Press, 2005.

——, and Mercer, Joyce. *Lives to Offer: Accompanying Youth on Their Vocational Quests*. Cleveland: Pilgrim Press, 2007.

Bartky, Sandra Lee. *Femininity and Domination: Studies in the Phenomenology of Oppression*. New York: Routledge, 1990.

Blodgett, Barbara J. *Constructing the Erotic: Sexual Ethics and Adolescent Girls*. Cleveland: Pilgrim Press, 2002.

Bonhoeffer, Dietrich. *Letters and Papers from Prison*. London: SCM Press, 1953.

Bordo, Susan. *Unbearable Weight: Feminism, Western Culture, and the Body*. Berkeley: University of California Press, 1993.

Bourdieu, Pierre. *The Logic of Practice*. Cambridge: Polity Press/Basil Blackwell, 1990.

Brown, Lyn Mikel. *Girlfighting: Betrayal and Rejection Among Girls*. New York: New York University Press, 2003.

———, and Gilligan, Carol. *Meeting at the Crossroads: Women's Psychology and Girls' Development.*Cambridge, Mass.: Harvard University Press, 1992.

Brueggemann, Walter. "Covenanting as Human Vocation." *Interpretation,* 1979, *33*(2), 126.

———. *Texts Under Negotiation: The Bible and Postmodern Imagination.* Minneapolis: Fortress Press, 1993.

Brumberg, Joan Jacobs. *The Body Project: An Intimate History of American Girls.* New York: Vintage Books, 1998.

Cauce, Ana Mari, Hiraga, Yumi, Graves, Diane, Gonzales, Nancy, Ryan-Finn, Kimberly, and Grove, Kwai. "African American Mothers and Their Adolescent Daughters: Closeness, Conflict, and Control." In Bonnie J. Ross Leadbeater and Niobe Way (eds.), *Urban Girls: Resisting Stereotypes, Creating Identities.* New York: New York University Press, 1996.

Collins, Patricia Hill. *Black Feminist Thought: Knowledge, Consciousness, and the Politics of Empowerment.* Boston: Unwin Hyman, 1990.

Cornell, Drucilla. *Transformations: Recollective Imagination and Sexual Difference.* New York: Routledge, 1993.

Davis, Patricia H. *Counseling Adolescent Girls.* Minneapolis: Fortress Press, 1996.

Debold, Elizabeth, Brown, Lyn Mikel, Weseen, Susan, and Brookins, Geraldine Kearse. "Cultivating Hardiness Zones for Adolescent Girls: A Reconceptualization of Resilience in Relationships with Caring Adults." In Norine G. Johnson, Michael C. Roberts, and Judith Worell (eds.), *Beyond Appearance: A New Look at Adolescent Girls.* Washington, D.C.: American Psychological Association, 1999.

Devlin, Rachel. *Relative Intimacy: Fathers, Adolescent Daughters, and Postwar American Culture.* Chapel Hill: University of North Carolina Press, 2005.

DeZolt, Denise M., and Henning-Stout, Mary. "Adolescent Girls' Experiences in School and Community Settings." In Norine G. Johnson, Michael C. Roberts, and Judith Worell (eds.), *Beyond Appearance: A New Look at Adolescent Girls.* Washington, D.C.: American Psychological Association, 1999.

Durkheim, Émile. *The Elementary Forms of the Religious Life.* New York: Free Press, 1965.

Erkut, Sumru, Fields, Jacquiline P., Sing, Rachel, and Marx, Fern. "Diversity in Girls' Experiences: Feeling Good About Who You Are." In Bonnie J. Ross Leadbeater and Niobe Way (eds.), *Urban Girls: Resisting Stereotypes, Creating Identities.* New York: New York University Press, 1996.

Fowler, James W. "Faith/Belief." In Rodney J. Hunter (ed.), *Dictionary of Pastoral Care and Counseling.* Nashville: Abingdon Press, 1990.

————. *Faith Development and Pastoral Care.* Philadelphia: Fortress Press, 1987.

————. *Stages of Faith: The Psychology of Human Development and the Quest for Meaning.* San Francisco: HarperOne, 1981.

Gilligan, Carol. *In a Different Voice: Psychological Theory and Women's Development.* Cambridge, Mass.: Harvard University Press, 1982.

————, Lyons, Nona, Hanmer, Trudy J., and Emma Willard School. *Making Connections: The Relational Worlds of Adolescent Girls at Emma Willard School.* Troy, N.Y.: Emma Willard School, 1989.

————, and Rogers, Annie. "Reframing Daughtering and Mothering: A Paradigm Shift in Psychology." In Janneke van Mens-Verhulst, Karlein Schreurs, and Liesbeth Woertman (eds.), *Daughtering and Mothering: Female Subjectivity Re-analyzed.* New York: Routledge, 1993.

————, Ward, Janie, Taylor, Jill McLean, and Bardige, Betty (eds.). *Mapping the Moral Domain: A Contribution of Women's Thinking to Psychological Theory and Education.* Cambridge, Mass.: Center for the Study of Gender Education and Human Development, Harvard University Graduate School of Education, 1988.

Hall, G. Stanley. *Adolescence.* New York: Arno Press, 1969. (Originally published 1904.)

Jaffee, Lynn, and Mahle Lutter, Judy. "Adolescent Girls: Factors Influencing Low and High Body Image." *Melpomene Journal,* 1995, *14*(2), 14–22.

Johnson, Norine G., Roberts, Michael C., and Worell, Judith. *Beyond Appearance: A New Look at Adolescent Girls.* Washington, D.C.: American Psychological Association, 1999.

Kegan, Robert. *The Evolving Self: Problem and Process in Human Development.* Cambridge, Mass.: Harvard University Press, 1982.

Kindlon, Daniel J. *Alpha Girls: Understanding the New American Girl and How She Is Changing the World.* Emmaus, Pa.: Rodale, 2006.

LaRossa, Ralph. *The Modernization of Fatherhood: A Social and Political History.* Chicago: University of Chicago Press, 1997.

Lawrence-Lightfoot, Sara, and Davis, Jessica Hoffmann. *The Art and Science of Portraiture.* San Francisco: Jossey-Bass, 1997.

Leadbeater, Bonnie J. Ross, and Way, Niobe (eds.). *Urban Girls: Resisting Stereotypes, Creating Identities.* New York: New York University Press, 1996.

Media Education Foundation. *Reviving Ophelia: Saving the Selves of Adolescent Girls, with Author and Therapist Mary Pipher.* DVD produced by Susan Ericsson. Northampton, Mass.: Media Education Foundation, 2002.

Mercer, Joyce Ann. "Psychoanalysis, Parents, and God: Julia Kristeva on the Imaginary Father and Subjectivity." *Pastoral Psychology,* 2002, *50*(4), 243–258.

Montemayor, Raymond. "Family Variation in Parent-Adolescent Storm and Stress."*Journal of Adolescent Research,* 1986, *1,* 15–31.

Parker, Evelyn L. *The Sacred Selves of Adolescent Girls: Hard Stories of Race, Class, and Gender.* Cleveland: Pilgrim Press, 2007.

——. *Trouble Don't Last Always: Emancipatory Hope Among African American Adolescents.* Cleveland: Pilgrim Press, 2003.

Parks, Sharon Daloz. *Big Questions, Worthy Dreams: Mentoring Young Adults in Their Search for Meaning, Purpose, and Faith.* San Francisco: Jossey-Bass, 2000.

——. *The Critical Years: Young Adults and the Search for Meaning, Faith, and Commitment.* San Francisco: HarperOne, 1986.

Pipher, Mary Bray. *Reviving Ophelia: Saving the Selves of Adolescent Girls.* New York: Putnam, 1994.

Roof, Wade Clark, and McKinney, William. *American Mainline Religion: Its Changing Shape and Future.* New Brunswick, N.J.: Rutgers University Press, 1987.

Smith, Christian, and Denton, Melinda Lundquist. *Soul Searching: The Religious and Spiritual Lives of American Teenagers.* New York: Oxford University Press, 2005.

Smith, Wilfred Cantwell. *The Meaning and End of Religion.* New York: Macmillan, 1963.

Snarey, John R. *How Fathers Care for the Next Generation: A Four-Decade Study.* Cambridge, Mass.: Harvard University Press, 1993.

Stern, Daniel N. *The First Relationship: Infant and Mother.* Cambridge, Mass.: Harvard University Press, 2002.

Surrey, Janet. "The Mother-Daughter Relationship: Themes in Psychotherapy." In Janneke van Mens-Verhulst, Karlein Schreurs, and Liesbeth Woertman (eds.), *Daughtering and Mothering: Female Subjectivity Re-analyzed.* New York: Routledge, 1993.

Tetlin, Patricia, Minnesota Women's Fund. *Reflections of Risk: Growing Up Female in Minnesota: A Report on the Health and Well-Being of Adolescent Girls in Minnesota.* Minneapolis: Minnesota Women's Fund, 1990.

Ward, Janie Victoria. "Raising Resisters: The Role of Truth Telling in the Psychological Development of African American Girls." In Bonnie J. Ross Leadbeater and Niobe Way (eds.), *Urban Girls: Resisting Stereotypes, Creating Identities.* New York: New York University Press, 1996.

Wilcox, William Bradford. *Soft Patriarchs, New Men: How Christianity Shapes Fathers and Husbands.* Chicago: University of Chicago Press, 2004.

Winnicott, D. W. *Playing and Reality.* New York: Basic Books, 1971.

THE AUTHOR

JOYCE ANN MERCER teaches practical theology at Virginia Theological Seminary, a seminary of the Episcopal Church, in Alexandria, Virginia. Her previous books include *Lives to Offer: Accompanying Youth on Their Vocational Quests,* coauthored with Dori Grinenko Baker (Pilgrim Press, 2007), and *Welcoming Children: A Practical Theology of Childhood* (Chalice Press, 2005). She is an ordained minister in the Presbyterian Church (U.S.A.) and a clinical social worker. Before moving to Virginia, Joyce taught at San Francisco Theological Seminary and at the Graduate Theological Union in Berkeley, California. She has served as a local church pastor, the chaplain of an adolescent chemical dependency treatment center, a mission co-worker in the Philippines, and a clinical social worker in children's hospitals in Atlanta and Minnesota. She is married to Larry Golemon, and they have two sons and a daughter.

INDEX

Femininity
  body images related to, 52–55
  defining gender stereotyping of, 48–52, 63
"Feminization of religion," 112
Fields, J. P., 56
Foucault, M., 2
Fowler, J. W., 13, 140n.5
Furnish, V. P., 90

G

Gender
  changing social construction of, 62–65
  family messages regarding, 66–69
  girl talk on, 69–72
  racial differences in perceptions of, 55–59
  reflections on meanings of, 72–74
  rejecting stereotypes of, 52–55, 63
  sexual double standards and, 45–46, 69
  on what it means to be female, 46–52
  See also Sexism
Gender differences
  in family division of labor, 66
  rejecting stereotypes of, 52–55
  trying to fit in notions of, 59–62
Gender identity
  changing social construction of, 62–65
  definition of, 142n.11
  racial differences and development of, 55–59
  relationship between behavior and, 63
  religious teachings on, 69–72, 90
  terminology related to, 58–59
Gender oppression
  continuing power of sexism and, 130–131
  religious teachings facilitating, 69–72, 90
"Gender outlaws," 61
"Gender positioning," 126, 146n.1
Gilligan, C., 92, 93
Girlfighting (Brown), 78
God
  abstraction and mystery of, 19–21

anthropomorphic, 140n.2
calls from, 33–35
as Creator, 125
embracing love of/relationship with, 16–19, 34
empathy of, 5–6
faith as gift from, 79
using "father" language to describe, 116–119
having "experience of," 24–25
male gender used to describe, 139n.1
metaphors and images used for, 16–17, 18
prayer used to connect with, 40–42
Godparenting, 12, 79
Golden Rule, 6–9
Good Mother image, 80–82
Good-enough mothering, 121–122
Great, good, good-enough father images, 119–122

H

Hall, G. S., 86
Holy Communion, 37–38, 43
Hope, 40–42
How Fathers Care for the Next Generation (Snarey), 122
Hughes, J., 119

I

Identity
  class as, 138n.9
  construction of sense of self or, 78
  gender, 55–59, 62–65, 69–72
Inclusion markers, 37–38
Interviewees
  Abbie, 63, 69
  Althea, 25, 41–42, 72
  Alyssa, 20, 35, 108–110
  Andrea, 32, 66–67, 120–121
  Brenda, 26, 57, 70–71, 121
  Carol, 117, 118
  Chelsea, 28, 31
  Courtney, 29, 40–41
  Deana, 22
  Denise, 45–46
  Elaine, 1, 25, 117
  Ellen, 32, 54, 80–81
  Jan, 61–62, 65, 67, 110–111